"Tell Newt to Shut Up!"

PRIZEWINNING *WASHINGTON POST*
JOURNALISTS REVEAL HOW REALITY
GAGGED THE GINGRICH REVOLUTION

David Maraniss and Michael Weisskopf

A TOUCHSTONE BOOK
PUBLISHED BY SIMON & SCHUSTER

To Linda, Andrew, and Sarah
and to Judith and Skyler

TOUCHSTONE
Rockefeller Center
1230 Avenue of the Americas
New York, NY 10020

Design by Irving Perkins Associates

Manufactured in the United States of America

10 9 8 7 6 5 4 3 2 1

Library of Congress Cataloging-in-Publication Data is available.

ISBN 0-684-83293-3

Contents

Crying Time

NEWT GINGRICH WAS sobbing like a child, heaving and shaking. He had lost it, his aura of certitude gone with the tears. This was not the persona he had presented in public all year. He had sounded so sure of himself. He spoke in sweeping sentences bursting with adjectives and adverbs that rendered his world oversized and absolute. Enormous. Classic. Grotesque. Tremendous. Totally. Frankly. Unequivocally. Extraordinarily. Explicitly. He wore these words as epaulets of power. He used them to define his surroundings, though they revealed more about him than anything else. He would enter a room and see uncertainty and dispatch his words to clarify the scene. If he encountered disorder his words would reorder everything into lists. Frankly, here are the first three things we need to think about. Here are four extraordinary books you must read. These are the five enormously important principles to follow. He never reached the top in academia, and he never served in the military, yet his self-image was that of the heroic soldier-scholar who could inculcate his troops and lead them into battle. That was House Speaker Gingrich in 1995; or so it appeared.

On the evening of December 6, at the close of another exhausting day near the end of his first year in power, Gingrich sat in the office of his chief of staff, Dan Meyer, trying to work out a legislative problem with three Republican colleagues from dairy states. There were no signs that anything was amiss. He brought his words and lists with him along with his favored management techniques in resolving internal disputes. The session at one point was interrupted by his secretary, who entered the room and handed him a note. Gingrich excused himself and retired to his back office, where he took the telephone near the rear window facing west into the darkness toward the intoxicating glow of the Washington Monument and Lincoln Memorial. It was a short conversation. When he finished, he returned to Meyer's office and resumed the discussion as if nothing had happened. Soon his wife, Marianne, who had just arrived at the Capitol, opened the door, caught sight of her husband, and said, "I understand you have some news about our future."

"Oh, yeah," said Gingrich. He turned to the others in the room. "I didn't want to bother you guys. That call was Nancy Johnson." Johnson chaired the House Committee on Standards of Official Conduct, which had just completed a long day of voting on a list of ethics complaints filed against Gingrich by his Democratic adversaries. Most of the charges had been thrown out, he said. A special counsel would investigate whether he had violated the law by using tax-deductible donations to finance a college course he taught in Georgia. But that was all. The other charges brought nothing more than a verbal slap on the wrist for violating the spirit of House rules. There was a long silence. Finally someone said it sounded like a victory for the speaker.

"Yeah," Gingrich said, his voice choking. "But no one knows what my wife and kids have gone through for two and a half years of charge after charge after charge."

Tears welled in Gingrich's eyes. The mood in the room suddenly changed. His aides looked away and thought they should leave him alone. Marianne moved to embrace him, crying herself. Steve Gunderson of Wisconsin, one of the dairy state legislators and an old Gingrich ally, rose from his chair and hugged them both. Gingrich could no longer hold back his emotions. He began sobbing uncontrollably.

It was not just the ethics decision that made him lose his composure that night, Gingrich explained later. It was everything. It was a year's accumulation of burdens from commanding his conservative revolution. It was the self-inflicted wounds. The petulance of his comments about being slighted by President Clinton during the long flight to Israel and back on Air Force One for the funeral of Yitzhak Rabin. The fact that his own allies were telling him to shut up. The drubbing he was taking in the polls and in the press. The grind of holding together his increasingly obstreperous rank-and-file. The struggle with an "old establishment" unhappy because he was "trying to change their world."

And, as much as anything, it was the pressure of the end game battle with Bill Clinton over the seminal issue of the Republican Congress, a budget bill that would cut the growth of Medicare and Medicaid, diminish the role of government, and balance the federal budget in seven years. Only hours earlier, using a pen with which LBJ had signed Medicare into law thirty years before, Clinton had vetoed Congress's version of a balanced budget measure. With one stroke of the pen he had wiped out months of effort by the speaker and his troops.

Gingrich still thought that he would prevail, but now he saw the likelihood of a long, difficult fight ahead, one that might jeopardize his earlier accomplishments. His words had turned against him. He was heaving with sobs of fatigue that December night in the Capitol, overcome by what he had gone through and what awaited. It was a moment among friends where he could finally express "the totality of how hard it's been."

ONE

General Gingrich

SONNY BONO GOT it first. Before most professional image advisers and veteran Republican pols had a clue, the freshman congressman from Palm Springs anticipated what would happen. Newt Gingrich was rocketing into a new realm, and he seemed to have no idea how different and dangerous it would be. It mattered little that he had prepared himself to be Speaker of the U.S. House of Representatives since his college days, or that he had spent thousands of hours with managers at Delta, Coca-Cola, Ford, and the Army studying how large institutions operated. Everything he had learned about leadership from examining the careers of FDR, Churchill, and Reagan was secondary now to one unavoidable fact that a mustachioed little guy who crooned "I Got You Babe" with Cher intuitively understood when others did not.

Bono issued his warning on the morning the world changed: January 4, 1995. Sonny's first day as congressman. Newt's first day as speaker. The revolution was already in full, dizzying swirl. Newt was marching from meeting to interview to speech with the bearing of an overstuffed field general, surrounded by the hubbub scrum of aides, photographers, and press hacks. As he and Bob Dole, majority leader of the Senate, were leaving a CBS Morning News interview in the old Agriculture Committee Room in the

Longworth House Office Building, Bono approached them. The singer-cum-pol was scheduled to be the network's next guest, but before he went on the air he had a word of advice for his new boss. What Newt was feeling now, he said, was what Sonny felt the first time he cut a hit record. You dream and dream and dream and then all of a sudden it happens so fast.

"You're a celebrity now," he told Gingrich. "The rules are different for celebrities. I know it. I've been there. I've been a celebrity. I used to be a bigger celebrity. But let me tell you, you're not being handled right. This is not political news coverage. This is celebrity status. You need handlers. You need to understand what you're doing. You need to understand the attitude of the media toward celebrities."

Gingrich barely listened. This was the biggest day of his life. No time for alarms, especially not from Sonny Bono.

"Yeah," he said distractedly. "We'll get around to that."

THE rest of it had been plotted for years, relentlessly, even when it seemed preposterous.

Back in 1979, during his freshman term in Congress, Gingrich had pestered the National Republican Congressional Committee (NRCC) brass into letting him run their long-range planning committee. He had experience at this sort of thing, he told them: he had chaired a similar panel at West Georgia College during his teaching stint there. He visited the NRCC offices day and night, proposing one grand idea after another. The joke at committee headquarters was that they had a wall lined with filing cabinets loaded down with "Newt's Ideas." One lonely cabinet in the corner was labeled "Newt's Good Ideas." But his one all-consuming idea never changed. Someday there would be a Republican majority in the House with him at the top. His mission throughout the next decade was to crumble the pillars of Democratic rule while constructing a new framework for his own rise.

He alternately worked the positive and negative. Positive: Build the Conservative Opportunity Society of congressmen who shared his vision. Negative: Use the group to tear down Democratic leaders like House Speaker Jim Wright. Positive: Train state and local Republican troops for a new majority through GOPAC, a national political action committee that Gingrich developed as a conservative farm club. Negative: Pound the Democrats for abuse of power and treat misdeeds such as the House Bank check-bouncing episode like the biggest scandals in American history. The public saw only the incendiary Newt, tossing hand grenades from the House back bench, saying anything to rile the opposition. Those images captured part of his dual character. They would linger long after he tried to transform himself into a sober leader, making it doubly difficult for him whenever he regressed back to his old outrageous self. The positive Newt, the visionary party builder, operated largely out of public view. The press rarely covered internal minority party politics in those days. Interest in House Republicans was as low, as one adviser lamented, "as whaleshit on the bottom of the ocean."

Gingrich's years of tactical maneuvering took a profound turn in the spring of 1993. By then he was minority whip, ostensibly second-in-command to Minority Leader Bob Michel of Illinois, yet heir apparent and de facto general of his party in the House. Michel still ran the floor operation. He loved the floor, he thought the day-to-day action was the central function of Congress and all the rest was foolish nonsense. He left the larger strategic questions to Gingrich, a most unusual whip who seemed indifferent to what was moving on the floor. Gingrich was consumed by bigger ideas. Improbable though it still seemed, he thought the time had come to prepare for Republican rule and solidify his future leadership team.

Operating on a simple principle—"What is the smallest group that can effect things?"—he decided on a group of five. Dick Armey of Texas, the former college professor who had just been elected chairman of the Republican Conference, someone Gingrich regarded as his equal in intelligence and ambition. Conference secretary Tom DeLay, another Texan and an aggressive operator who was developing his own power base and, like Armey, could be a threat unless he was brought into the team.

Bob Walker of Pennsylvania, Gingrich's loyal sidekick and skilled parliamentarian. And Bill Paxon of New York, chairman of the NRCC, a cheerleader sort who brought business resources to the table.

At Gingrich's call throughout the next two years, the gang of five gathered regularly late at night in the back room of the Hunan Dynasty restaurant on Pennsylvania Avenue to "discuss the notion of taking over the House." Gingrich was maneuvering on two strategic levels at once. He was a politician with many allies but few close friends among his colleagues. From his analysis of how large corporations handled change, he understood that to transform the House he had to build not only tactical relationships but partnerships. The explicit purpose of the Hunan Dynasty meetings was to plot the takeover of the House, but Gingrich's private intent was to form a partnership with his four colleagues that would enhance his power when and if they seized control. When the time came that they reached a crisis, Gingrich hoped, they would "instinctively know how to move as a unit." And his team would "gain momentum by training and delegating and trusting."

There was some inevitable tension within the group. Armey, the lumbering, backwater intellectual, had been a loner most of his life. Walker, the friendly, Howdy Doodyish former teacher who seemed comfortable sporting a pen protector in his breast pocket, and DeLay, a Texas popinjay with the icy chuckle of a hit man, were opposite personality types, and both were interested in the same job as Newt's whip when and if they reached power. But over time they bonded, just as Gingrich had hoped. Their staffs joked that they all pricked their thumbs and became blood brothers. They took on a private nickname—"Just Us Chickens." As in, "We're meeting tonight, Just Us Chickens."

By the spring of 1994, Gingrich had the team where he wanted it. Each chicken had a specific mission. Gingrich would travel the country campaigning for the new troops he would need to seize power. Paxon would take the message to corporate America. Armey would prepare the policy platform for the revolution—the ten-point plan that became known as the Contract with America.

Walker and DeLay would run the floor operation together, sublimating their ambition even as they ran against each other for the job of whip. The chickens would hold a competition to see who could raise the most money for Republican challengers. Their assistants had melded as well into what was called a unified staff. Ed Gillespie, Armey's communications director, worked in tandem with Tony Blankley, Gingrich's press secretary. Kerry Knott, Armey's chief of staff, was teamed with Dan Meyer, who ran Gingrich's operation. While this teamwork approach seemed to spread the responsibility around, it also accomplished exactly what Gingrich wanted, allowing him to maintain complete control.

As early as April of that year, seven months before the off-year congressional elections, Knott, acting at the direction of Armey and Gingrich, quietly began compiling a black book on the mechanics of taking over the House. How do you hire a clerk? Who do you get to fire? Who literally turns on the lights? How do you choose committee chairmen? Can you change the number and structure of committees? How do you make sure sensitive legislative documents are preserved and not shredded by departing Democrats? Who gets what offices? Out of power for forty years, the Republicans had no precedents to fall back on. Thousands of things that the House Democratic leadership did as a matter of habit remained a complete mystery to the Republicans.

The planning grew more intense month by month. The day after Mike Synar, a popular Oklahoma Democrat, was defeated in a September primary by a little-known challenger who had successfully linked Synar to President Clinton, Gingrich turned to Dan Meyer and said, "I always believed we had a shot. Now it's getting more serious. We've got to make sure we have our act together in case anything happens." A few days later, Joe Gaylord, Gingrich's longtime nuts-and-bolts political adviser, turned to him as they were jetting across country and said, "You better start preparing for the speakership." The conventional wisdom still held that the Democrats would lose fifteen to twenty-five seats in the House, not enough to lose control. Gaylord projected a more dramatic result. He said the Republicans would gain fifty-two. The chickens spent the rest of the fall expecting to come home to roost. They took over precisely as Gaylord predicted. Fifty-two seats.

GINGRICH prided himself as a manager. He loved the jargon. He had all these little sayings. He broke any mission into VSTP: Vision, Strategy, Tactics, Projects. He called himself the Chief Executive Officer and Chairman of the Board and Dick Armey his Chief Operating Officer. He sent his staff down to the U.S. Army Training and Doctrine centers at Fort Monroe, Virginia, and Fort Leavenworth, Kansas, to study management techniques. They learned how to lay out branches and sequences TRADOC-style: If we get to this point, what do we do here? How do we sequence it out? They adopted the Army's use of After Action Reviews to study what had gone wrong or right on legislative initiatives. Gingrich brought in Fortune 500 executives from the Business Roundtable to share dinner with him in the Speaker's Dining Room and tutor him in the intricacies of downsizing a large institution. Take it further than you think you can go, executives from General Electric, General Motors, Eastman Kodak, and du Pont told him. The problems never ease up, they said.

But one issue was left untouched in all his planning: Himself. There was no discussion of the transformation of Newt Gingrich into a celebrity, a symbol, and a big juicy target for the revolution's adversaries.

Early on, there was some disquiet among the troops when Gingrich signed a contract to receive a $4.5 million advance to write a book published by HarperCollins, which was owned by Rupert Murdoch, the media baron who was one of the speaker's political benefactors and who had sensitive legislation pending before the House. But it took some time for the complaints to reach Gingrich. When he called around town, his informal advisers told him it was no problem. Bill Bennett, the former education secretary who had made a bundle on his own book, a compendium of value-laden children's stories, said Gingrich should take the contract. So did Vin Weber, the former Minnesota congressman who had been

Gingrich's longtime ally. Haley Barbour, chairman of the Republican National Committee, offered the first words of caution, saying the hefty book deal might confuse the troops. Then during the Thanksgiving holiday, Gingrich started to hear from members of his leadership team. Paxon, Walker, and Susan Molinari of New York all urged him to drop the deal. "You can't do this, it looks like you're cashing in!" said Molinari.

Nicks and dents in General Gingrich's armor came one after another. On the very day he took office, he had to deal with the quote that his mother had whispered to Connie Chung—Between you and me, Newt once said Hillary Rodham Clinton was a bitch. The old flamethrower image reappeared twice more in the first days of his regime. Once he declared that the Clinton White House was rife with drug abusers. Another time he offered the notion that more orphanages might help slow the disintegration of America's social order. House GOP Conference Chairman John Boehner of Ohio was stunned by the orphanage comment. "Orphanages?" he thought to himself. "I haven't heard that word in fifteen years." God, can't you get him to stop this stuff? members started asking Boehner and others in the leadership team.

Still Gingrich kept talking. His speakership was built on talk. It was not coincidental that the favored guests in the Capitol during his first week in office were radio talk show hosts. They were stationed everywhere, in Statuary Hall, in the basement—one radio gabmeister was even housed in a small room across the hall from Dan Meyer's office in the speaker's suite.

Gingrich talked. Every day from January through March, he held a daily briefing in the Capitol. He would not shut up. He believed that if he "poured enough energy into substance," meaning that if he concentrated his attention on the Contract with America and a balanced budget, the focus on him would seem insignificant in contrast. But he had made himself inseparable from policy. He was a celebrity, as Sonny Bono understood. There were other Republicans in the House who would try to shape events and burst into the news. But in the end they were all subordinate to Newt. It seemed that he was the revolution and the revolution was him.

Let the Lobby Boys In

THE DAY BEFORE the Republicans formally took control of Congress, Tom DeLay of Texas strolled into a meeting in the rear conference room of his commodious new leadership suite on the first floor of the Capitol. A dapper, snuff-dipping backslapper with the persona of a pledge leader in a southern frat house, DeLay was soon to be sworn in as majority whip of the foremost fraternity lodge in the land, the House of Representatives. He now saw before him a lineup of pals who had eased his rise to the top. They were lobbyists representing some of the most powerful companies in America, assembled in his office on mismatched chairs amid packing boxes, an unplugged copying machine, and constantly ringing telephones. DeLay was delighted to see them. He could not wait to get started on what he considered the driving mission of his political career: the demise of the modern era of government regulation.

Since his arrival in Washington a decade earlier, DeLay, a former exterminator who had made a living killing fire ants and termites on Houston's wealthy west side, had been seeking to eradicate federal safety and environmental rules that he felt placed excessive burdens on American business. During his ascent to power in Congress, he had befriended many industry lobbyists who shared his fervor. Some of them were in his office now, as energized as he was by a sense that their time was at hand. The session inaugurated an unambiguous collaboration of political and commercial interests, certainly not uncommon in Washington but remarkable this time for the ease and eagerness with which the allies combined. Republicans championed their legislative agenda as an answer to popular disaffection with Congress and the federal government. But it also represented a triumph for business, a form of political revenge for the multinational corporations and small business groups who now found themselves full partners of the Republican leadership in shaping congressional priorities after years of playing a defensive role when the Democrats controlled Congress.

The campaign launched in DeLay's office on January 3, 1995, was quick and initially successful. It resulted in a lopsided vote by the House for what once seemed improbable: a thirteen-month halt to the sorts of government directives that had been established to ensure a safe workplace and unpolluted environment but were considered oppressive and counterproductive by many businesses. This antiregulatory effort was separate from provisions in the Contract with America aimed at rolling back federal regulatory and environmental laws, but it was related to them in scope and antigovernment intent. The first draft of the moratorium plan, outlined that day in DeLay's office by legislative ghost writer Gordon Gooch, an oversized, folksy Texan who lobbied for energy and petrochemical interests, called for a hundred-day moratorium on rulemaking while the House pushed through the comprehensive antiregulatory planks in the Contract.

Other lobbyists in DeLay's inner circle argued that Gooch had been too timid, perhaps not having fully adjusted to the new era of Republican friends in high congressional places. Over the next few days, several drafts were exchanged by the corporate agents. Each new version sharpened and expanded the moratorium bill, often with the interests of clients in mind — one provision favoring California motor fleets, another protecting industrial consumers of natural gas, and a third keeping alive Union Carbide Corporation's hopes for altering a Labor Department requirement. As the measure progressed, the roles of legislator and lobbyist blurred. DeLay and his assistants guided industry supporters in an ad hoc group whose name, "Project Relief," sounded more like a Third World humanitarian aid effort than a corporate alliance with a half-million-dollar communications budget and a battalion of lobbyists. On key amendments, the coalition provided the draftsmen. And once the bill moved to the House floor, lobbyists hovered nearby, tapping out talking points on a laptop computer for delivery to Republican floor leaders.

Many of Project Relief's 350 industry members had spent the past few decades angling for a place of power in Democratic governing circles and had made lavish contributions to Democratic campaigns, often as much out of pragmatism as ideology. But now they were in the position of being courted and consulted by newly empowered Republicans dedicated to cutting government regulation and eager to share the job. No one was more openly solicitous in that respect than DeLay. Democrat David Obey of Wisconsin once said of the tough-talking Texan that "he never met a public interest regulation he didn't hate." It was a description that DeLay, after six terms in Washington, was reluctant to dispute. In his white-hot vocabulary, the Environmental Protection Agency was "the Gestapo of government pure and simple." DeLay considered his partnership with Project Relief a model for effective Republican lawmaking, a fair fight against Democratic alliances with labor unions and environmentalists. "Our supporters are no different than theirs," he said of the Democrats. "But somehow they have this Christ-like attitude that what they are doing is protecting the world when they're tearing it apart." Turning to business lobbyists to draft legislation made sense, according to DeLay, because "they have the expertise."

But the alliance with business and industry was not without peril. It was based on the assumption, which DeLay above all others took to heart, that the Republican majority had been swept into power with a mandate to weaken environmental regulations. That premise grew more tenuous as the year progressed. Starting with the regulatory moratorium, every environmental issue the Republicans tackled became increasingly troublesome. The House's hard-line posture turned into a source of embarrassment for party moderates who had considered environmental protection a bipartisan issue. Internal polls eventually revealed that an anti-environmental mandate did not exist. More than 55 percent of Republican voters came to the conclusion that their own party could not be trusted to protect the environment. On a larger political scale, the effects were even more damaging. President Clinton's slow but steady recovery throughout 1995 was based in part on his ability to define himself in opposition to the Republicans on a set of specific issues, the environment prime among them.

The Republicans also found themselves walking a fine line, and occasionally tripping over it, as they tried to balance their antiregulatory zeal with the populist aura they had developed in 1994 to carry them into power. There was a general consensus that the public was angry at Washington; but what part of Washington, represented by what symbols: the frustration of bureaucratic red tape or the coziness of legislator and lobbyist at a back-room lunch? Were the Republican attacks on environmental regulations in the name of the average citizen or on behalf of the corporate elite? Were they addressing the concerns of reform-minded Perot voters, other independents, and disenchanted blue-collar Democrats who had voted Republican in 1994—or were they paying back the traditional business interests that had long dominated the Republican Party? Could they serve both causes at the same time?

William Kristol, a key Republican analyst whose frequent strategy memos helped shape the conservative agenda, maintained at the start of the year that the way Gingrich's revolutionaries resolved those questions would determine their prospects for consolidating congressional power. "If they legislate for special interests," he said, "it's going to be hard to show the Republican Party has fundamentally changed the way business is done in Washington."

It was not until much later that Gingrich came to understand the dilemma. Early in the year, he ceded the battle over environmental regulations to lieutenants like DeLay.

* * *

AFTER graduating from the University of Houston with a biology degree in 1970, Tom DeLay, the son of an oil-drilling contractor, found himself managing a pesticide formula company. Four years later he was the owner of Albo Pest Control, a little outfit whose name he hated but kept anyway because a marketing study said it reminded consumers of a well-known brand of dog food. DeLay transformed Albo into "the Cadillac of Houston exterminators, serving only the finest homes." But his frustration with government rules increased in concert with his financial success. He hated federal worker safety rules, including one that required his termite men to wear hard hats when they tunneled under houses. And the Environmental Protection Agency's pesticide regulations, he said, "drove me crazy." He viewed the ban on DDT as excessive and the one on Mirex as even worse. A chemical effective in killing fire ants, Mirex was initially labeled a dangerous carcinogen by federal bureaucrats. By the time they changed their assessment a few years later, it was too late: Mirex had gone out of business.

The cost and complexity of regulations, DeLay said, got in the way of profits and drove him into politics. "I found out government was a cost of doing business, and I better get involved in it." He arrived in the Texas legislature in 1978 with a nickname that defined his mission: "Mr. DeReg." Seven years later he moved his crusade to Washington as the congressman from Houston's conservative southwest suburbs. He publicized his cause by handing out Red Tape Awards for what he considered the most frivolous regulations. But it was a quixotic enterprise, hardly noticed in the Democrat-dominated House, where systematic regulation of industry was seen as necessary to prevent the business community from putting profit over the public interest and to guarantee a safe, clean, and fair society. The greater public good, Democratic leaders and their allies in labor and environmental groups argued, had been well served by government regulation. Countless highway deaths had been prevented by mandatory safety procedures in cars. Bald eagles were flying because of the ban on DDT. Rivers were saved by federal mandates on sewerage.

DeLay nonetheless was gaining notice in the world of commerce. Businessmen would complain about the cost of regulation, an expense that the government has estimated amounts to $430 billion a year passed along to consumers. They would cite what they thought were silly rules, such as the naming of dishwashing liquid on a list of hazardous materials in the workplace. Every Tuesday for a full year before the Republican takeover, DeLay ate lunch with a changing cast of Washington corporate agents, thirty or forty altogether, who met in the Capitol Hill boardroom of the Independent Insurance Agents of America. The luncheons served as the embryo of Project Relief—lobbyists for tobacco, telecommunications, pharmaceuticals, food and beer distributors, freight, securities, and health insurance. They pushed for regulatory relief, and they saw DeLay as their point man.

The mutual benefits of that relationship were most evident in 1994 when DeLay was running for Republican whip. He knew the best way to accumulate chits was to raise campaign funds for other candidates. The large number of open congressional seats and the lineup of strong Republican challengers offered him an unusual opportunity. He turned to his network of business friends and lobbyists. "I sometimes overly prevailed on" these allies, DeLay said later. In the 1994 elections, he was the second-leading fund-raiser for House Republican candidates, behind only Gingrich. In adding up contributions he had solicited for others, DeLay said, he lost count at about $2 million. His persuasive powers were evident in the case of the National-American Wholesale Grocers Association PAC, which already had contributed $120,000 to candidates by the time DeLay addressed the group in September 1995. After listening to his speech on what could be accomplished by a pro-business Congress, they contributed another $80,000 to Republicans and consulted DeLay, among others, on its distribution.

The chief lobbyist for the grocers, Bruce Gates, would be recruited later by DeLay to chair his antiregulatory Project Relief. Several other business lobbyists played crucial roles in his 1994 fund-raising and also followed Gates's path into the antiregulatory effort. Among the most active were David Rehr of the National Beer Wholesalers Association, Dan Mattoon of BellSouth Corporation, Robert Rusbuldt of Independent Insurance Agents of America, and Elaine Graham of the National Restaurant Association. At the center of the campaign network was Mildred Webber, a political consultant who had been hired by DeLay to run his race for whip. She stayed in regular contact with both the lobbyists and more than eighty GOP congressional challengers, drafting talking points for the neophyte candidates and calling the lobbyist bank when they needed money. Contributions came in from various business PACs, which Webber bundled together with a good-luck note from DeLay. "We'd rustle up checks for the guy and make sure Tom got the credit," said Rehr, the beer lobbyist. "So when new members voted for majority whip, they'd say, 'I wouldn't be here if it wasn't for Tom DeLay.' "

DeLay, in return, hosted fund-raisers in the districts to draw business support and brought challengers to Washington for introduction to the PAC community at the Capitol Hill Club. One event was thrown for David M. McIntosh, an Indiana candidate who had run the regulation-cutting Council on Competitiveness in the Bush administration under fellow Hoosier Dan Quayle. McIntosh won, and was rewarded with the chairmanship of the House regulatory affairs subcommittee. He hired Webber as staff director. It was with the lopsided support of such Republican freshmen as McIntosh that DeLay swamped two rivals and became the majority whip of the 104th Congress. Before the vote, he had received final commitments from fifty-two of the seventy-three newcomers.

It was a classic triumph of old-fashioned politics that impressed Newt Gingrich even as it alarmed him. DeLay was a team player, but he also had his own independent power base. In attaining the whip's position, he had defeated Gingrich's oldest and closest friend in the House, Robert Walker of Pennsylvania. If DeLay went too far in his deregulatory fervor, Gingrich might have a hard time controlling him. The distance between the two men was evident even at early meetings of the leadership. Others in the room noticed that Gingrich would get impatient whenever DeLay piped up.

*   *   *

THE idea of Project Relief first surfaced in the Tuesday lunches DeLay shared with lobbyists. After the November 1994 elections, he pushed them to "link up their resources with ours." Although business groups were consulted by Democrats during their reign, they normally were ushered in for comment after legislation had been drafted. DeLay embraced lobbyists more openly as part of what he called an "interactive" family of conservatives in which "you can work for each other and get a common goal." He needed a resourceful team, he said, to root out "oppressive bureaucrats" and the "arrogance of the leftist elite." Within weeks, Project Relief had grown into one of the most diverse business groups ever formed for specific legislative action.

Leaders of the group, at their first post-election meeting, discussed the need for an immediate move to place a moratorium on federal rules. More than four thousand regulations, some of the toughest and costliest ever, were due out in the coming months, before the Republican House could deal with comprehensive antiregulatory legislation. In the pipeline were labor standards to reduce the physical strains of the workplace; more stringent rules for meat inspection to prevent *E. coli* bacteria and other foodborne illnesses; and a requirement to install and operate sophisticated devices on manufacturing plants for monitoring hazardous air pollutants, a requirement that the petrochemical industry estimated would cost up to $1 billion.

DeLay agreed with the business lobbyists that a regulatory "timeout" was needed. He wrote a letter to the Clinton administration dated December 12, 1994, asking for a hundred-day freeze on federal rulemaking. The request was rejected two days later by a midlevel official who described the moratorium concept as a "blunderbuss." DeLay then turned to Gooch to write legislation that would do what the administration would not. At the January 3, 1995, meeting in DeLay's office, Paul C. Smith, lobbyist for some of the nation's largest motor fleets, criticized Gooch's draft because it excluded court-imposed regulations. He volunteered to write the next draft and came back with a version that addressed the concerns of his clients. Under court order, the Environmental

Protection Agency (EPA) was about to impose an air pollution plan in California that might force some of Smith's clients—United Parcel Service (UPS) and auto-leasing companies—to run vehicles on ultra-clean fuels, requiring the replacement of their fleets. Smith removed the threat with a stroke of his pen, extending the moratorium to cover court deadlines. A buttoned-down lawyer who learned the skill of bill drafting as a young House staffer, Smith also helped Webber add wording in a later amendment that extended the moratorium from eight to thirteen months.

Peter Molinaro, a mustached lobbyist for Union Carbide, had a different concern: He wanted to make sure the moratorium would not affect new federal rules if their intention was to soften or streamline other federal rules. The Labor Department, for example, was reviewing a proposal to narrow a rule that employers keep records of off-duty injuries to workers. Union Carbide had been fined $50,000 for violating that rule and was eager for it to be changed. Molinaro importuned the drafters to find a way of exempting "good regulations." For his part, Gooch wanted to ensure that the routine, day-to-day workings of regulatory agencies would not be interrupted by a moratorium. His clients, including Dow Chemical and Hoechst-Celanese, rely on the Federal Energy Regulatory Commission to make sure that natural gas and oil, used in their production processes, flow consistently and at reasonable rates. In his own mind, Gooch thought he was functioning as a legislative assistant to his old friend DeLay. But working for the revolution was not without commercial benefit.

"I'm not claiming to be a Boy Scout," Gooch said later. "No question I thought what I was doing was in the best interests of my clients."

ON the first day of February 1995, fifty Project Relief lobbyists met in a House committee room to map out their vote-getting strategy for the moratorium bill. Their keynote speaker was DeLay, who laid out his basic objective: Make it a veto-proof bill by lining up a sufficient number of Democratic co-sponsors. They went to work. Kim McKernan of the National Federation of Independent Business read down a list of seventy-two House Democrats who had just voted for the GOP balanced budget amendment, rating the likelihood of their joining the antiregulatory effort. The Democrats were placed in Tier One for gettable and Tier Two for questionable. Every Democrat was assigned to a Project Relief lobbyist, often one who had an angle to play.

The nonprescription drug industry chose legislators with Johnson & Johnson plants in their districts, such as Ralph M. Hall of Texas and Frank Pallone, Jr., of New Jersey. David Thompson, who lobbies for a major construction company based in Greenville, targeted South Carolina congressman John Spratt. Federal Express, with its Memphis hub, took Tennessee's John Tanner. Southwestern Bell Corporation, a past campaign contributor to Blanche Lambert Lincoln of Arkansas, agreed to contact her. Retail farm suppliers picked rural lawmakers, including Charles Stenholm of Texas. The trucking lobby went after Bill Brewster, whose state of Oklahoma is a major trucking center and highway interchange.

When they were not buttonholing Democrats themselves, the lobbyists turned on the pressure by remote control. The American Trucking Associations asked thousands of members in Democratic districts to round up the support of their congressmen. The Financial Executives Institute, representing corporate treasurers and controllers, went a step further, supplying sample letters to its subscribers. Gooch urged his network of energy and petrochemical clients to get out the word through their own lobbyists in Washington and their corporate newsletters. "If you feel like you're oppressed by bureaucrats," he told them, "here for the first time and maybe the last, is your chance to see fundamental changes in the way the federal government regulates. Don't let it go by."

As the moratorium bill reached the House floor, the business coalition proved equally potent. Twenty major corporate groups advised lawmakers on the eve of debate, February 23, that this was a key vote, one that would be considered in future campaign contributions. McIntosh, who served as DeLay's deputy for deregulation, assembled a war room in a small office just off the House floor to respond to challenges from Democratic opponents. His rapid response team included Paul Smith, the motor fleet lobbyist, to answer environmental questions; James H. Burnley IV, an airline lobbyist who had served as transportation secretary in the Reagan administration, to advise on transportation rules; and UPS lobbyist Dorothy Strunk, a former director of the Occupational Safety and Health Administration (OSHA), to tackle workplace issues. Project Relief chairman Gates and lobbyists for small business and trucking companies also participated.

When Republican leaders were caught off guard by a Democratic amendment or alerted to a last-minute problem by one of their allies, Smith would bang out responses on his laptop computer and hand the disk to a McIntosh aide who had them printed and delivered to the House floor. A last-minute snag arose over immigration concerns of Lamar Smith of Texas. Forty-five minutes later, the war-room lobbyists had persuaded Smith's aide that the problem could be resolved with what is known in legislative parlance as a colloquy—a discussion on the House floor of the bill's intent. From the laptop came a scripted colloquy that McIntosh and Smith read into the record largely verbatim.

The final vote for the moratorium was 276 to 146, with fifty-one Democrats joining DeLay's side. The support exceeded the original hopes of Project Relief leaders. As McIntosh watched the tally, DeLay wandered over and grabbed the freshman's right hand. "I've been waiting for this to happen for sixteen years," DeLay said. One week later, he appeared before a gathering of a few hundred lobbyists, lawmakers, and reporters in the Caucus Room of the Cannon House Office Building to celebrate the House's success in voting to freeze government regulations and, in a pair of companion bills, curtail them. He stood next to a five-foot replica of the Statue of Liberty that was wrapped from neck to toe in bright red tape. Next to him stood Bruce Gates, the chairman of Project Relief. At the same moment, working in tandem, the legislator and the lobbyist pulled out scissors and jubilantly snipped away.

THREE

A Moderate Turns Right

THE CONGRESSIONAL OFFICE of Bill Goodling, Room 2263 of the Rayburn Building, is a quaint and cozy place straight out of the 1950s, with the ambiance of a small-town Pennsylvania school principal's den. Portraits of Ike at Gettysburg grace the front wall. In the far right corner stands a century-old upright piano from the North Wales Music Company, a clangingly out-of-tune instrument that nonetheless brings the congressman great comfort when he pounds out Methodist church hymns alone at midnight. Behind his desk sit rows of potted African violets, which the grandfatherly Goodling fondly refers to as his "children."

This old-fashioned hideaway is hardly the first spot one would look in search of leading characters in the House Republican Revolution, with its New Age rhetoric and antigovernment fervor. Yet it was in Goodling's antiquated office and in the nearby quarters of the committee he runs that one of the most compelling conflicts of the Republican House's first one hundred days was staged. Goodling played a leading role in pushing one of the main provisions of the Contract with America—a role that tested his political soul as he struggled, at the twilight of an obscure career, to attain and hold power in an institution dominated by young partisans pushing him from the right. In a larger sense, his saga foreshadowed the message and policy troubles that would plague Gingrich's House later in the year.

Since he entered Congress in 1975 after a career as an educator in the heart of Pennsylvania Dutch country, Goodling had earned a reputation on the House Education and Labor Committee as a moderate who worked in bipartisan fashion to protect the federal role in food and nutrition programs for needy children, infants, and pregnant mothers. It was a natural extension of his paternalistic personality: taking care of his children, just as he had as father, public school teacher, administrator, and cultivator of African violets. He was anything but a conservative firebrand: during the years when Newt Gingrich was throwing rhetorical bombs at the congressional establishment, Goodling was enjoying his role as an insider. He loved to reminisce about long-ago back-room conferences with Hubert Humphrey, one of the founding fathers of federal food programs. ("Muriel forces me to eat red beets and I hate red beets!" Goodling recalled the jolly Minnesotan confessing to him once as they hammered out legislation on nutrition requirements for school lunches.)

But when the Republicans took power, Goodling suddenly became chairman of a committee that had been repopulated with antigovernment conservatives and went by a new-fangled Third Wave name: Economic and Educational Opportunities. His first assignment from Speaker Gingrich and Majority Leader Armey was to carry out one of the most controversial missions in the Contract with America. They directed him, as part of a larger welfare overhaul, to dismantle and send back to the states the very nutritional programs that he had long championed. Goodling's personal dilemma—how to respond to the pressures of the conservative leadership without repudiating his past legislative career—illuminated a larger morality play within the House: The struggle of the Republican majority to maintain the populist appeal of antigovernment rhetoric without appearing to abandon the young, the poor, and the elderly, and without seeming to acquiesce to corporate interests.

On one side, pushing hard for more power and freedom, were the nation's newly ascendant Republican governors, who visited Washington so often to lobby for block grants that they virtually set up a shadow White House two blocks from Goodling's congressional office. On another side were major cereal companies, infant formula manufacturers, agribusinesses, and fast-food giants for whom the federal retreat from the nutrition field presented an opportunity for new markets and less government regulation. And finally there were the most vulnerable members of society, whose needs historically had been met by a bipartisan coalition in Congress under the precept that hunger in America was a nationwide crisis too dire to be left to the states. It was a federal responsibility.

AT first, Dale Kildee could not imagine that his friendly adversary Bill Goodling was changing. This must be a technical error, the veteran Democratic congressman from Michigan thought to himself when he entered the Opportunities Committee room one day late in February 1995 for the vote to send the nutrition programs back to the states. The bill as the Republicans had drafted it left out any requirement that states use competitive bidding procedures when buying infant formula from the major companies supplying the Special Supplemental Food Program for Women, Infants, and Children (WIC)—a nutritional program assisting 7 million people that had an effective record limiting infant mortality and premature births.

In the early days of the program, infant formula was bought at market prices. Since Congress began requiring competitive bidding in 1989, the prices had dropped dramatically, saving more than $1 billion in 1994 alone and nearly $4 billion over the previous five years. All of those savings were put back into the program, meaning that more needy infants and pregnant women could be served. When he noticed that competitive bidding had been left out of the Republican bill this time, Kildee assumed that it was an unintentional omission, so he drafted an amendment restoring it. He took the amendment to Chairman Goodling, confident that it would be accepted quickly. But Goodling's reaction was cool and distant. Go "work it out" with Hoekstra, he told Kildee, referring to Peter Hoekstra, a second-term congressman from western Michigan, one of the youthful free enterprise Republicans on the committee who was gaining stature as a confidant of Speaker Gingrich.

Nothing was to be worked out. Hoekstra had a strong distrust of the federal government and was one of the staunchest proponents of devolving power back to the states. "Philosophically," he said, "it was a no-brainer" that Congress should eliminate federal mandates whenever possible—even the competitive bidding requirements that had saved money. Hoekstra's philosophical commitment in this case coincided with the desires of one of the major corporations in his congressional district—Gerber Products, a Fremont-based company that is the nation's largest manufacturer of baby foods and is WIC's leading supplier of infant cereals. Unlike in the infant formula field, competitive bidding is not required of infant cereal suppliers, but the government seemed to be moving in that direction and Gerber wanted to maintain the status quo. The company lobbied hard against competitive bidding requirements in the infant cereal industry and had consulted with Hoekstra in the drafting of the legislation.

When Kildee's amendment came to a vote in committee, it was defeated on a near party-line vote, with only one Republican supporting it, Marge Roukema, a veteran moderate from New Jersey. Roukema said later that she was not even aware that competitive bidding was omitted from the Republican bill until the deliberations that day. In the committee room after the vote, she asked several Republican members seated near her why they had done what they had done. Their responses, she said, were shrugs of the shoulders and the words, "We trust the governors."

ONLY a few blocks from the land of Economic and Educational Opportunities sits a venerable Republican redoubt called the Capitol Hill Club, where members of Congress mix easily with corporate lobbyists and important visitors from back home. It was there, sitting in stuffed chairs beneath crystal chandeliers and oil paintings of GOP stalwarts, that key committee members met with the big winners in the transfer of money back to the states, Republican governors such as John Engler of Michigan, Tommy Thompson of Wisconsin, Christine Todd Whitman of New Jersey, Pete Wilson of California, and William Weld of Massachusetts. These governors had been important allies of Gingrich and his revolution from the start. Shortly after the 1994 elections that brought the GOP to power, they gathered at a retreat in Williamsburg, Virginia, and struck their bargain for the year. Realizing that Congress would have far less money to offer them for social programs, the governors agreed to support the funding reductions as long as they were ceded the power to decide when and how the money would be spent. "We couldn't give them more money, so we had to give them something else," said Republican Congressman Steve Gunderson of Wisconsin.

In the food and nutrition programs, the governors got most of what they wanted from Gingrich and his troops, but not all. Their bid for a single enormous block grant for all the programs was rebuffed by Goodling and Duke Cunningham of California, the nutrition subcommittee chairman, who thought they could define the terms of the transfer better with two separate block grants. But the governors did receive more power and flexibility to run the school lunch and WIC programs. For years, some governors and corporate interests had bristled at regulations that they considered too intrusive—from dictating the amount of sugar allowed in WIC foods to when and where soft drinks could be sold in public schools.

Michigan's Governor Engler, who would visit Gingrich's office so often over the year that he would seem like a member of the speaker's staff, was among the loudest critics of federal rules and regulations. At a committee hearing he derided them as a "crazy quilt." As in the case of fellow Michigander Hoekstra and the Gerber connection, there were narrower economic consequences of devolution important to Engler as well, in this case involving another major manufacturing constituent—the Kellogg Company. The cereal giant from Battle Creek had fought for years to modify a federal limit on sugar content that excludes Raisin Bran, one of its top-selling products, from the nutrition program for needy pregnant women and their young children. Purchased separately, raisins and bran both fall within the sugar standard, but combined in Kellogg's Raisin Bran they represent twice the amount that government nutritionists consider healthy in a single serving.

Until the Republican Revolution in Washington, Kellogg's efforts to revise the standard and compete in the $285-million-a-year market for WIC adult cereals had proved futile—"like hitting a brick wall," in the words of company vice president James Stewart. Now Kellogg saw an opportunity to accomplish on the state level what it could not do with the federal government. The firm employed John Ford, son of the former committee chairman, retired Democratic Congressman William D. Ford of Michigan, to head its lobbying effort. Kellogg also enlisted the support of Governor Engler and his staff, who pressed the committee to keep the block grants silent on the question of nutritional standards.

Not even the harshest critics of block grants predicted the total abandonment of sound nutrition standards by the states. But the devolution process would create a long-sought opening for many food industries to carve out larger niches in the annual $8.5 billion school lunch and WIC programs. Financially strapped state governments and part-time legislatures, many nutritionists argued, are ill-equipped to make sound public health judgments and can be more easily swayed by corporate lobbyists. The return of nutrition programs to the states would lift federal controls on the lunchtime sale of junk food in school cafeterias—a prospect that several corporate food giants anticipated. Coca-Cola, which in 1994 fought off a legislative effort to extend the junk-food ban to all high school grounds, began showing signs of interest. As the devolution legislation moved through the House, the company's law librarian called the National Association of School Cafeteria Personnel for a breakdown of state laws on soft drink sales in schools.

Also at stake in the transfer of power to the states was one of the cornerstones of the war on hunger, a 1946 requirement that school lunches provide one-third of the recommended dietary allowance of protein, vitamins, and minerals. The dietary guideline is intended to assure at least one healthy serving a day of milk, vegetables, grain, fruit, and meat for the 25 million children in the program. Federal agriculture officials were planning to add limits soon on fat, saturated fat, and sodium for school lunches. With standards defined by states, food companies and agricultural interests with special regional standing would have more power, some nutritionists contended. "You could find a battle going on in a state legislature over what drinks to serve at school lunch," said Lynn Parker, a child nutritionist for the Food Research and Action Center. "In a dairy state, it might go one way. If soda interests are strong, it could go another way. Whatever way it goes, it may not be fought out on the grounds of what's best for the kids."

Goodling and his Republican colleagues on the Opportunities Committee expressed confidence that the states would demonstrate sound nutritional and financial practices in dealing with the programs. Their critics were less certain, citing the recent history of the WIC program as evidence. The infant formula industry, dominated by Mead Johnson & Co. and Ross Products Division of Abbott Laboratories, had raised prices a dozen times from 1981 to 1989, gobbling up more and more of the funds allocated for cereals, milk, eggs, cheese, juice, and other foods in the program. After competitive bidding was imposed nationwide, with Goodling's support, prices dropped enough to feed another 1.5 million needy women and infants. In defending the decision to drop competitive bidding language from the devolution legislation, Goodling said governors would be "idiots" not to impose it themselves. But as a recent case in California showed, states are not always as cost-conscious or resistant to industry pressures. When California's competitively awarded contract with Ross Products expired in December 1994, it sought to extend the deal without rebidding it. The Agriculture Department said no, forcing a new round of solicitations and a new low bid—half the price of the old deal. The state ended up saving $22 million a year.

"If ever there was a case of narrow corporate interests over broad societal interests, this is it," said Robert Greenstein, head of the Center on Budget and Policy Priorities.

FEW issues all year created as much furor as the child nutrition bill, and none was more mishandled by the Republican communications team. Gingrich's legislative technique was to try to package change in a larger moral framework and invent simple, nonthreatening phrases to describe it, then have the words repeated so often they became axiomatic. It worked smoothly for most of the Contract with America, but failed in the case of children and food. It was unclear how important this failure was at the time. In retrospect, it was obvious. The food fight marked the first time that Democrats, who had been foundering since the election, developed a strong voice on social issues and clearly had the public on their side. Gingrich's effort to slip in radical change came up short.

At the center of the dispute was the rhetorical use and manipulation of one word: cuts. In their proposal to abolish federal food programs and send them back to the states, the Republicans were planning to increase the funding of the programs by 4.5 percent a year. But the normal growth rate for those programs that would be followed if there were no changes would be 5.2 percent. Was this a cut? The Democrats said it was, and pounded away on that theme: School lunch programs were being cut. Stories reached the front page and network news broadcasts about how vulnerable many children would be under the draconian Republican program. There were reports of southern schools where more than 90 percent of the students ate their only nutritious meals in the cafeterias. The block grant notion, which the Republicans thought of as a reasonable change that would save about $2 billion over five years, was becoming an unmitigated public relations disaster.

The low point came during a briefing on the issue in February when Gingrich and his aides realized midway through the session that they were suffering from a communications breakdown. No one from Goodling's committee had attended the briefing to rebut Democratic charges that they were taking food out of the mouths of needy children. Before the session was over, Goodling and Majority Leader Armey were dispatched to the House Press Gallery, but it was too late. Democrats were waving ketchup bottles, evoking an embarrassing moment from the Republican past when President Reagan's administration had claimed that ketchup was a vegetable. Now it was coming back to haunt them again: Republicans don't care about people. President Clinton also seized the public relations advantage. He ventured out to an elementary school in suburban Washington, sat down for a cafeteria lunch, and slammed the Republicans for "cutting this program" as a way of financing tax cuts for the rich, exploiting another element of the Contract with America.

By early March, White House pollster Stanley Greenberg was reporting a 20 percent increase in people who thought the Republican Revolution was too extreme, the first noticeable rise since the election. Gingrich, dismayed, chastised his staff and placed a call to the dean of Republican imagemakers, Michael Deaver. "The Democrats, every time you say cut, scream blood. 'It's going to throw people out on the streets. The lines of the Depression are back.' All that kind of stuff," Deaver said. "Demagogic. But it works." Gingrich and his troops were thinking that the world had changed more than it had. "You've got to be sensitive," he told them. "If you're going to do something, you have to explain how this is going to help people. Whatever the biggest fears are, you have to address those."

It was a lesson the revolutionaries forgot, and a problem they would face again.

THERE is a touch of mythology to the notion that politicians in the old days dealt with hunger and nutrition issues on a totally cooperative bipartisan basis. Though moderate Republicans like

Bill Goodling and his ideological predecessors, Charles Goodell of New York and Al Quie of Minnesota, often co-sponsored legislation drafted by Democratic staffers in the old Education and Labor Committee, the Democrats had the power and used it ruthlessly. "We rolled the Republicans every time," recalled John Kramer, once an aide to former chairman Adam Clayton Powell, Jr., and now dean of Tulane law school. "We had no fairness. We just screwed them." In the 1970s, after Democratic staffers for the two leading nutrition advocates in the Senate, Hubert Humphrey and George McGovern, developed the WIC program, the Nixon and Ford administrations occasionally sought to curtail it by impounding or cutting funds, a trend that continued in the 1980s under Reagan. All those efforts backfired: court challenges consistently left the program with more money than it had before.

Despite these power plays over legislation and funding, however, there was a broad bipartisan consensus that fighting hunger in America was too essential to be left to the states. It was in fact Richard Nixon, guided by Daniel Patrick Moynihan, his urban affairs adviser at the time, who delivered a seminal speech on the subject in December 1969 at the opening of his White House Conference on Food, Nutrition, and Health. "Until this moment in our history as a nation, the central question has been whether we as a nation would accept the problem of malnourishment as a national responsibility," Nixon said. "That moment is past. . . . Speaking for this administration, I not only accept the responsibility—I claim the responsibility."

From the time he entered Congress two decades ago, Bill Goodling accepted that responsibility as well. He already had a reputation for compassion and a deep interest in children and nutrition. As superintendent of Spring Grove School District in southeastern Pennsylvania, he ate lunch every day in the cafeteria with his students. When the truck from Harrisburg pulled up with vegetables and meats from the federal commodities program, he helped carry the food down to the freezer in the basement of the administration building. He often helped the cafeteria cooks plan the weekly lunch menus in his outer office. When the mother of one of his students died, he taught the young man how to cook dinner for himself and his father. When morale was low in the administration building, Goodling would drive down to his father's orchard on the old Susquehanna Road and bring back a bushel of apples for everyone.

Along with running the apple orchard, Goodling's father, George Goodling, served in Congress himself for six terms. When he retired, his son Bill replaced him. The small-town educator transferred his interests to the broader stage of the Education and Labor Committee. He became known as one of the staunchest defenders of the nutrition and school lunch programs on the Republican side of the aisle. In 1982, he was his party's chief co-sponsor of a resolution opposing a Reagan administration proposal to send nutrition programs back to the states through block grants. Three years later, when conservative Republicans in the House were considering ways to trim the budget and broached the possibility of cutting back on the national school lunch program, Goodling swiftly killed the idea before it advanced beyond the discussion stage. According to Tom Humbert, then a budget aide to Jack Kemp of New York, Goodling called him one day. "Please come and see me," Goodling said. Humbert soon appeared in Goodling's office, where he found the congressman tending his African violets. "Mr. Humbert," Goodling said, "I hear that you are considering cutting the school lunch program. That would be a very bad idea!"

This same Tom Humbert, who came from Goodling's home district, returned to York County in 1992 and ran against the incumbent in a heated three-way general election contest—a race that Humbert and others saw as the beginning of Goodling's political transformation. Humbert ran as an independent, challenging Goodling from the right. Along with support from Kemp, Humbert was also endorsed by Dick Armey, who considered Goodling too moderate and tied to the old ways of doing business in Washington. Humbert and the Democratic candidate, Paul Kilker, both blasted Goodling for his role in the House Bank scandal after it came out that year that Goodling had hundreds of overdrafts and was among the twenty-two "worst abusers" of the system.

In his moment of need, Goodling received a visit and timely endorsement from an unlikely friend, the leader of House conservatives, Newt Gingrich. Then the minority whip, Gingrich traveled up to Capital City Airport in York County and staged a press conference with Goodling at which he took issue with Armey and other conservatives who had broken ranks to support Humbert. The independent campaign had "done the party a great disservice," Gingrich said. In supporting Goodling, Gingrich had to swallow all the harsh statements he had made earlier about the House Bank episode, which he had once called "the largest institutional scandal in the history of the U.S. House." The major transgressors, Gingrich had said, deserved nothing but "severe retribution." But Gingrich had made those statements when he thought it was purely a Democratic scandal, before it was revealed that some Republicans were among the heaviest overdrafters (and that Gingrich himself had thirty overdrafts). Goodling, Gingrich explained during his visit to the district, was known for his decency and was merely a victim of "the way the Democrats ran the Bank."

That visit formed a bond between Goodling and Gingrich that grew stronger after the election, which Goodling won. Goodling supported Gingrich in his rise to power, and Gingrich elevated Goodling to the chairmanship after the revolution, even though some members of the leadership team grumbled about the selection, questioning whether the soft-spoken Pennsylvanian was sufficiently energetic and conservative. Former aides on the committee's minority staff detected a noticeable shift in their boss's politics as he linked his fortunes to Gingrich. Even his moderate colleague on the committee, Steve Gunderson, said he noticed Goodling moving to the right in 1994. Gunderson attributed it to positioning by new members of the staff to gain favor with Gingrich and Armey, who had reconciled with Goodling after the 1992 election. The word in Congress and around the nutrition community was that Goodling was ordered by the leadership to "carry the water" for the committee's portion of the Contract with

America. By the time he took over the panel, he had little choice in any case.

Opportunities, once a haven for moderates, had been transformed into a stronghold of free enterprise true believers, many of them recruited by their intellectual leader, Armey, who served on the panel before becoming majority leader. The sense of these committee conservatives, as expressed by Cass Ballenger, a garrulous good ole boy from North Carolina, was "to get rid of Washington whenever and wherever we can." Ballenger had a personal interest in trying to remove the federal bureaucracy from the school lunch program. He and his wife founded the Community Ridge Day Care Center in his hometown of Hickory, a federally subsidized program that served school breakfasts and lunches. The paperwork for reimbursements, Ballenger said, went through Raleigh, then Atlanta, and finally Washington—a process that meant Ballenger's center "has to underwrite" the meals for a month. He would get his money quicker, the congressman said, with the federal government out of the way. The Opportunities panel, by Ballenger's account, was attracting free enterprise "wild men" and "nuts" who had various similar frustrations with the federal bureaucracy.

Goodling was not considered part of that crowd yet. He prevented efforts by archconservatives on his committee to curb the school lunch program more drastically. Hoekstra and Ballenger wanted to limit the increase in the block grants to half the 4.5 percent that eventually was allowed. Goodling also rebuffed the attempt by governors and committee members to lump all the programs in one block grant. "I said, 'No way, José,' to that one," the chairman boasted. The two block grant proposals pushed through Goodling's committee marked a significant cutback nonetheless, a reduction of $6.6 billion over five years, according to the Agriculture Department. But Goodling said that the states deserved the opportunity to run the programs—"We can't dictate everything," he said—and that the reduced bureaucracy would lead to savings that could be passed along to those who need the programs.

The sight of Bill Goodling leading the way for the end of federal involvement in the antihunger programs surprised some longtime colleagues. It seemed as though to some extent he was being forced to swallow something that he did not find entirely palatable. His training as an educator might have helped there, too. Once, while eating lunch with first-graders at one of the Spring Grove elementary schools, Goodling found himself staring down at a steaming heap of cooked spinach. He hated cooked spinach. But there was a little boy gazing at him, and he felt that he had no choice but to "push this slimy stuff down my throat to show that I'm eating everything that's on the plate."

FOUR

John Kasich's Dream Machine

THE ABIDING OBSESSION of John Richard Kasich grew ever more intense until it finally seeped into his subconscious. He began dreaming about the federal budget. His budget dreams were invariably ugly. When he fell asleep, his restless mind encountered the same nocturnal furies—fellow members of Congress who appeared before him red-faced and screaming: "How could you do this to us! We didn't know about this!"

As chairman of the House Budget Committee, which undertook the historic but precarious task of attempting to slash programs to balance the federal books by the year 2002, Kasich's confrontations, real and imagined, were getting nastier day by day in May 1995. He had reached a critical moment in his congressional career, a time when his obsession, his dreams, and the fate of his party became inextricably linked. The high-profile House votes on the Contract with America were over by then. Every point in that conservative agenda except term limits had passed the House, but many of them were stalling in the Senate and the early momentum was dissipating. It was obvious to Speaker Gingrich that to bring about significant legislative change, he would have to rely heavily on the balanced budget bill. That also meant relying more on John Kasich. The fate of the revolution would depend on how the irrepressible mailman's son and Gingrich protégé handled the pressures, the degree to which he lived up to his reputation as an honest broker willing to take on turf-conscious colleagues and special interests traditionally aligned with the Republicans.

Kasich was anything but the green eyeshade sort, more of a human bottle rocket than a patient numbers nerd, but he had a peculiar attraction to the arcane art of the budget. He had been drafting budgets aimed at eliminating the federal deficit since 1989, though those earlier efforts had been brushed aside by the White House or congressional leadership or both. This time he had the strength of the House Republican Revolution behind him. Gingrich had not only supported Kasich's effort but gave it a crucial kickstart. At a news briefing on Valentine's Day, during a period when the Contract with America's provision calling for a constitutional amendment to balance the budget seemed endangered in the Senate, the speaker issued an unequivocal declaration: The House would move forward no matter what happened, pass a bill that balanced the budget in seven years, and push it through Congress.

The declaration of seven years made Kasich and his budget aides nervous. It was one thing to put that number in the constitutional amendment, a document without real numbers in it, but another to have to deal with it in reality. At that point Kasich and his staff were working on a five-year budget—the traditional time span for federal budget projections—that would get them on what was called a "glide path" to balance in seven years. But they were not yet comfortable with the substantial amount of program cuts they would have to make in the sixth and seventh years to reach zero. At a leadership meeting over dinner in Gingrich's office on February 15, Kasich and his aides expressed concern that a seven-year balanced budget would require Medicare cuts "unlike any this town has ever seen before." Kasich was hoping to have more flexibility. "Who said we have to do seven years?" he asked.

Gingrich remained adamant. This was a critical point for the revolution, he said. They could go forward with what they really believed, or "start accommodating to Washington realities." There was no choice: Go forward. Kasich pressed the question one last time at a leadership meeting on February 21. "Is this etched in stone?" he asked. Gingrich, exasperated, put it to a vote. "All in favor of having it etched in stone raise your hands." Every hand went up except the budget chairman's.

But from that moment on, no member of the House was more committed to seven years than Kasich. In March and April he pushed his staff and his budget committee to find a way to get to zero in seven years. By the night of May 2, he had crafted a plan that had the unanimous approval of the Republicans on his committee. The next day he was ready to take it to the full House Republican membership. At three o'clock that afternoon, he bounced out of his congressional office in the Longworth Building and slipped into the front passenger seat of Ohio colleague Dave Hobson's Olds 88 for a fifty-minute drive through the northern Virginia countryside to Leesburg, Virginia, where Gingrich and his troops were staging a retreat, regrouping after their first vacation break of the year. The central mission of the retreat was to coalesce around a master plan for the tough budget fights that loomed ahead. Kasich was his usual bundle of nervous energy on the trip to Leesburg, a condition only exacerbated by questions from a backseat passenger, moderate Nancy Johnson of Connecticut, who worried about the budget plan's treatment of Medicare and Medicaid, foreshadowing problems to come.

The gathering was Kasich's coming-out party of sorts. The morning after his arrival at the retreat, he took the floor to describe his budget plan. But as he roamed the aisles, praising and cajoling his brothers and sisters in a style that reminded one witness of "Brother John's Traveling Salvation Show," it did not take long for him to notice the first sign of trouble: The Aggies were missing. House Republicans from rural districts, known on Capitol Hill as "Aggies," had essentially boycotted the opening of Kasich's presentation to caucus among themselves in another part of the conference center. Earlier that morning, they had found out from their leader, Pat Roberts of Kansas, chairman of the House Agriculture Committee, that the Budget Committee proposal cut farm subsidies by $11.7 billion. It was too much, said Roberts, a fellow so attached to the farm constituency that he maintained a tote board on the wall of his Capitol Hill office recording the ups and downs of wheat, corn, milo, and cattle on the Dodge City Daily Markets. Roberts wanted the number cut to single digits.

The shadowplay with the Aggies marked the opening of an important two-week stretch for Kasich that culminated in the House's historic vote approving a measure intended to balance the federal books by the year 2002. On the surface, the budget enterprise seemed to benefit from a remarkable display of party unity. Kasich's plan sailed through the committee and the House floor with only one dissenting vote. But behind the scenes, the boyish budget chairman's we-can-work-it-out motto was stretched to the limit by several powerful factions: the Aggies; a competing group of urban members known as "the Road Gang"; as well as defense hawks and corporate tax break defenders, all of whom threatened to withhold support until their needs were met.

The money in dispute—a relatively few tens of billions of dollars amid $1.4 trillion in savings—seemed almost marginal in comparison with massive cuts in Medicare, job training, science, and education that would become the fields of battle months later when the balanced budget fight turned into a fierce partisan contest with President Clinton. But the internal political considerations at play in May went to the heart of the Republican Party's relationships with key constituencies and its ability to survive as a congressional majority. Relenting here and bargaining there, Kasich attempted to ensure that no faction would suffer or benefit out of proportion to the rest. It was a process that reminded him of a sensitive moment in his own life, after his elderly parents were killed in a traffic accident. "It's kind of like when Mom and Dad go, and you've got to go into the house and figure out who gets what," he said. "You don't want to send an appraiser in there to appraise everything and divide it up, if you're going to do things in a humane and decent way. But you kind of get a sense, well, I'll get this couch, and, does that kind of measure up to this over there? Yeah, I think so. And that's kind of the way you do it."

Kasich occasionally found himself pulling back from his personal preferences. The plan he brought to Leesburg, in keeping with his own priorities, was a spending blueprint guided more by frugality than politics. But when his plan challenged a few too many idols of the Republican Party, he retreated in favor of the somewhat more subtle dictates of Speaker Gingrich, who was paying more attention to the political consequences of each budget decision.

The site of the Republican retreat was Xerox Document University, a campus of concrete so reminiscent of a penitentiary that some congressmen took to calling it "Lorton West" in honor of the nearby prison. It seemed an appropriate arena for the kind of hostility Kasich occasionally encountered. While the Aggies were caucusing in protest, he heard first from Duke Cunningham, a former Vietnam fighter ace from California who was the prototype for the Tom Cruise character in the movie *Top Gun*. Cunningham was seething at fine print in Kasich's budget that saved $25 billion by shaving 1.5 percent from the cost-of-living allowances built into military pensions. It was more of a betrayal, Cunningham told the gathering, than "George Bush moving his lips."

"At twelve years, I put in my papers to get out of the Navy," Cunningham told his colleagues. "I was flying the Indian Ocean. The skipper came back and said, 'Duke, you only have eight years to go. You can do that standing on your head. Here's what your retirement benefits will be.' I said, 'Wait a minute, if I retire at forty-five or fifty and live for another thirty-five years, I'll get zero because of inflation.' He said, 'You'll have the same buying power as now because of the cost-of-living allowance.' I bought into it. That's a contract."

When the public works section was presented, Bud Shuster of Pennsylvania, chairman of the Transportation and Infrastructure Committee, countered Kasich's salesmanship with a threat. The proposal to phase out Amtrak and freeze mass transit projects was

"a transportation disaster," Shuster stated. He said it would be difficult to guarantee votes for the budget among the Road Gang unless
Kasich agreed to take the transportation trust funds "off budget,"
giving Shuster's committee autonomy over $32 billion in gaso-
line and airline ticket taxes. Shuster, whose congressional office
is adorned with replica signs of Bud Shuster Highway, a stretch
of road running down from Altoona, had been seeking full control of the trust funds for years and had calculated that the budget
resolution might be his best opportunity.

The suit-and-tie contingent from the Ways and Means Committee also had a gripe. Led by Chairman Bill Archer of Texas,
several members of the tax-setting panel took to the microphones
to challenge Kasich's proposal to save $25 billion by closing tax
loopholes for large corporate interests. Archer, who represents the
wealthy River Oaks section of Houston, home to the corporate
elite, argued that the illustrative "corporate welfare" cuts in the
budget plan—taking away tax credits for pharmaceutical companies operating in Puerto Rico and eliminating deductions for advertising costs—were in essence tax hikes, which he said he would
not tolerate on his watch.

WHEN the general session was over, the private negotiations began.
Kasich decided quickly that he would have to relent in some areas.
Archer had outpositioned him by defining the corporate loophole
cutbacks as a tax increase. The long arm of the business lobby
had reached many members even out at Leesburg: the makeshift
communications room was filling up with faxes from corporate
agents trying to preserve the loopholes. The defense hawks also
got to Kasich that night. Duke Cunningham said he and his allies could not support a budget that capped cost-of-living allow-
ances. He brought out a letter with the signatures of more than fifty
Republicans asking that the cap be removed.

The leadership eventually agreed, and Kasich backed off. He
had mixed feelings about that decision. He considered the inflation cap a responsible cut, considering the precarious long-term

condition of the federal pension fund, and he privately told some Budget Committee colleagues later that he thought he had failed by caving in. On the other hand, in his larger mission to balance the budget, he felt that he had already won more than he had lost in his sometimes bitter confrontations with the defense hawks, especially Floyd Spence of South Carolina.

A courtly man of military bearing and soft Carolina tones, Spence represented a Columbia-based district that housed a Marine training center, a naval hospital, and bases for the Army, Air Force, and Navy. As chairman of the National Security Committee he was known as the Green Beret of defense spending, a reputation for toughness reinforced by his survival of a double-lung transplant in 1988. Spence regarded the Republican Revolution in the House as an opportunity to return to the full-throttle defense spending of the early 1980s. His view was shared by the defense industry, which contributed $3 million to congressional Republicans in 1994 and $1.2 million in the first six months of the nonelection year.

Early in the budget proceedings, Spence staked out the hawks' claim. In a February letter to Kasich, he asked for $125 billion more than President Clinton had budgeted for defense over the next five years. Kasich held a more cautious view of defense spending: He liked to say that careful fiscal stewardship could turn the Pentagon into a Triangle. On a Sunday news show, he had offered a less ambitious number than Spence's: adding $50 billion to Clinton's budget and freezing defense spending at $270 billion a year.

The conflict between the chief defense hawk and the lead deficit hawk prompted a meeting between the two men and Speaker Gingrich and the leadership. At that late February meeting, a frustrated Spence lashed out at Kasich for "siding with people who want to destroy our nation's defense." He was alluding to Kasich's campaign with liberal Democrats to limit production of the B-2 Stealth bomber. Kasich was stunned, but he remained silent for a minute, thought about what Gingrich had taught him about keeping cool, and finally replied: "Floyd, I respect you too much to respond." His restraint paid off. The meeting ended with Gingrich and the leadership sympathetic to Kasich. The defense number he promoted was never seriously challenged again by Republicans before it passed in the budget.

Within that larger context, Kasich felt, the cost-of-living dispute in Leesburg seemed like an area where he should defer. "Duke," he finally told Cunningham, "it's off the table."

Kasich's last negotiations at the retreat were with the head of the Aggie caucus, Pat Roberts. The farm subsidy issue had long been a point of contention among Republicans. Many conservatives, led by the Heritage Foundation and Majority Leader Armey of Texas, had called for the end of the "agricultural welfare state" of cash subsidies, price supports, and export promotion grants for the nation's 2 million farmers. But their cause had been losing some momentum. Kasich's committee began with informal discussions of cutting out $16 billion from the total $40 billion in farm subsidies over five years. Anything under that amount, hard-line anti-government reformers at Heritage argued, could be absorbed by the farm community without requiring the drastic transformation of agriculture subsidy policies that budget cutters desired.

But by the time Kasich got to Leesburg, political pressures had already forced the House agriculture number down to $11.7 billion. And Roberts wanted it much lower. He and Kasich met in the windowless communications room of the Xerox campus. Roberts, a lanky, balding Jayhawk with the sardonic sense of humor of a former newspaperman, arrived wearing Pat Boone – style tan suede shoes. He spread out a file of newspaper clippings and reports detailing the harm that further subsidy cuts might cause in farm country, stories that he had stirred up by holding sixteen hearings in rural America during the congressional break. The patter between Roberts and Kasich then switched back and forth between earnest argument and comic pantomime.

The farmers had already paid their dues, Roberts said, noting that because of previous cuts, the farm program was the only federal entitlement in which the numbers had been declining in the 1990s. He then interrupted his argument with a stage whisper: "Six" he hissed, meaning he would accept $6 billion in cuts.

Kasich laughed and whispered back, "No!"

These reports show cuts would cause declining land values, Roberts continued. "Six," he murmured again in a breathy exhale.

"How about this," Kasich whispered, scribbling out the number 10 on a piece of paper.

Roberts pulled out his most potent political argument, noting that thirty-four of the seventy-three freshmen Republicans come from farm country, primarily the South and West. "You don't want to shoot the troops with friendly fire," he said. This could cost the Republicans twenty to twenty-five seats next election.

Kasich later paraphrased the rest of Roberts's argument this way: "Look, Clinton goes off to Ag country and panders to all the farmers. He gets all the farm guys uptight because then the farm people start saying, 'Well, why are we getting the shaft out here? What's going on?' And the bankers are all uptight, they're freakin' out out here. And you're going to pull the rug out from under us!"

"Six," Roberts whispered.

"Turn that upside down," said Kasich.

They left the room with an unofficial agreement of $9 billion in cuts. Kasich got out of Leesburg with his budget relatively intact. He also brought back to Washington a present from Speaker Gingrich. It was a triangular nameplate of gold-speckled black marble with the commitment etched in stone:

Balanced Budget 2002.

WHEN Kasich formally opened the budget deliberations in his committee a week later, he alternately played the role of television game show host and earnest statesman. After gaveling the committee to order, he bounded from his high-backed chair and unveiled a National Debt Clock on the wall behind him, a digital contraption that blinked every second to add another $9,386 to the $4.7 trillion meter. Then he bragged about his Elvis Presley tie and compared the rarity of a balanced budget—a "zero sighting," he called it—to the infrequency of Elvis sightings. Soon he was more somber, evoking the stately ambiance of the committee room, with its pale green walls and oil portraits and chandeliers, as he declared that he and his Republican colleagues had united behind a "bold, innovative, and revolutionary" document that would erase the deficit in seven years. But behind his assertive exterior, Kasich was battling the same anxieties that haunted his dreams. He thought of the budget document as a painting, he explained: "And you just kind of say, this is a great painting, and you know they're going to take it and smash it and run over it with their cars."

The budget of the United States and Chairman Kasich might seem the unlikeliest of pairs, the immobile financial behemoth embraced by the wiry and fidgety politician. Kasich at forty-three was constitutionally incapable of keeping still, the antithesis of the placid bean-counter. Several friends said only half-jokingly that they often felt like giving him a shot of Ritalin, a drug used for hyperactive children. At a news conference with Gingrich and Armey one afternoon, Kasich kept bobbing and weaving in and out of camera range like a boxer about to move out of his corner, never once calming down for a motionless moment. His eyes blinked like a hummingbird's wings; thirty-six times in a minute, a time span when the more inert Armey blinked but twice. Kasich radiates so much energy that colleagues in the Ohio delegation, weary and looking for sleep, dread the thought of getting seated near him on the flights back to the Midwest.

His detractors in Congress would say that John Kasich's personality traits were more tiresome than fetching. He has been characterized by some as an argumentative gadfly, a man who devoted all his time and energy to cutting the government, finding pleasure in an act that can bring pain to others. He mocked the notion that his proposed cuts would bring pain. "Let's talk about job training programs," he once said to make the point. "Am I going to say, 'Okay, I just lost my job, but, honey, we don't have to worry about it because I just got myself a slot in the federal job training program'? Are you kidding?"

* * *

KASICH likes to say that he is from "the Rocks," slang for McKees Rocks, Pennsylvania, a blue-collar suburb on the western rim of Pittsburgh. It is a poetic place to be from, for a Republican who views himself as a populist and wants to distance himself from his party's old country club image. But in fact he grew up in the town next door, Stowe Township, which is like McKees Rocks in every way except its name is more leafy suburban. His roots are far from the country club, nonetheless. His Croatian grandfather was a steelworker and his father was the town mailman who drove his car to the post office every morning, gathered the letter bag, drove back home to the two-story brick house on Elizabeth Street, and walked the same daily route, befriending everyone along the way. John Kasich's energy and gregariousness came from his father, who was killed along with his mother in a traffic accident in 1987 when they were blindsided while pulling out of a Dairy Queen.

His persistence came from trying to compete on the dusty playing field at Fenton School as a scrawny little boy. "As a smaller guy I always had to give it everything," he said. The first reward for his persistence came late one fall evening in 1960, when he was eight and his mother drove him downtown for the celebration after the Pittsburgh Pirates won the World Series. Antsy little Kasich weaved his way through the crowd to get his baseball autographed by Bill Mazeroski, whose ninth-inning home run had beaten the Yankees. His nickname as a boy was "the Pope," in sarcastic recognition of his position as an altar boy and his desire to become a priest. For those who enjoy his effusive nature and boundless energy but worry that he sometimes loses direction, a story from his altar boy days captures his irascible sensibility. As Kasich later told the story, the priest once brought him up to the front to lead the parish in song. After telling the worshipers to turn to page 38 in the hymnal, he began belting out the hymn in his most earnest voice. After one stanza, he stopped and chewed out the congregation for not singing loud enough. "Now let's try it again. Sing it like you mean it!" the young Kasich bellowed.

When the service was over, an elderly woman approached him

and noted gently that the reason no one was singing was because
he had told them to turn to the wrong page.

Although his parents were Democrats, as were nine out of ten
residents of his hometown, Kasich became a Republican at Ohio
State University. It was the classic expression of campus bureaucracy—the registration line—that made him turn. He became a
Republican because he didn't like hassles, he didn't like "orders,
bureaucracy, rules, red tape, mazes, or anything else." His second
reward for persistence came during his university days, when he
became upset by a rule that made all the men in his dorm, even
those not responsible, pay a share of the cost for a broken window. He spent three weeks demanding to see the Ohio State president, Novice Fawcett. When he was finally granted an audience,
he heard Fawcett mention that he was going to see President Nixon
later that week. Kasich asked if he could come along. No, Fawcett
said, dumbfounded by the young man's brazenness. Then how
about taking a letter to the president for me? Kasich asked. The
administrator relented.

The letter so impressed Nixon that Kasich soon received a White
House invitation of his own. Budget cuts were always his political cause, going back long before his rise in Congress to his time
as an aide and later a senator in the Ohio legislature. He would
walk through the state administration buildings during the day,
see hundreds of people at desk jobs, and ask himself: "What are
they doing? What are they working on?" As a junior member of
the Ohio legislature, he began a tradition that he would take with
him to Washington: drafting detailed budgets as alternatives to
administration proposals.

After his election to the U.S. House in 1982—another reward
for persistence in a year when few other Republican challengers
succeeded—Kasich's eternal restlessness did not sit well with
some veterans in his party. He became known as a lone wolf, better at challenging authority than at negotiating. Until his rise to the
budget chairmanship, his most notable efforts involved building alliances with Democrats—first with Ronald Dellums of California
in fighting the B-2 Stealth bomber, and then with Tim Penny of

Minnesota in putting together a deficit reduction plan. Penny came to think of his unlikely sidekick as a tempestuous younger brother. "He can get frustrated at times, but he vents and gets it out of his system. If we ran up against a roadblock, he would say, 'We're dead in the water! What are we going to do?' A defeatist attitude would come through for a half-hour, but then he would get it out. It was a hoot."

Kasich's relationship with Gingrich was close but volatile. In private, Gingrich liked to call Kasich his "Heisman Trophy candidate," meaning he was the younger member with perhaps the most national potential. Gingrich also spent many private hours lecturing Kasich for acting stubborn, for occasionally rubbing other members the wrong way, and for seeming oblivious to the political consequences of his actions. Kasich, for his part, would speak reverentially of Gingrich one minute and make fun of him the next, especially when the speaker lapsed into his management lingo. "I became—to use Newt's word—a facilitator, I unlocked people," Kasich said facetiously once in describing a role he played mediating between the leadership and freshman Mark Neumann of Wisconsin, who had bucked the leadership in a key defense vote. Power, Kasich said, never intimidated him.

THAT does not mean that he always knew how to use power. House Republicans seemed united after their return from Leesburg, pushing through the measure intended to balance the budget by 2002 with only one dissenting Republican vote. But behind the scenes, the Aggies and the Road Gang were still clamoring for special attention. Kasich had been courteous but unaccommodating in his dealings with Shuster, so the leader of the Road Gang turned up the political pressure. As the chairman of the largest committee in Congress, with sixty members, Bud Shuster wielded the most obvious forms of political power: the ability to allocate projects in ways that the constituents of other lawmakers could readily see—roads, bridges, airports, subways—and a parallel ability to lure campaign contributions from affected industries. His own district, a hardscrabble swath of the Appalachian chain, had been awarded more money in special highway projects for the middle of this decade than all but three states. The transportation industry ranked second in corporate campaign funds in 1994, with $24 million, and contributed $2.8 million to the Republican Party in the first six months of 1995. Shuster alone received $246,000 from the industry in his past two uncontested reelection campaigns and $70,000 in his first six months as chairman.

It was his easy access to contractors that led Shuster to organize the Alliance for Truth in Transportation Budgeting. Comprising eighty business associations in the transportation field, the alliance pushed Shuster's agenda of taking the highway trust funds off budget where they could not be affected by budget-balancing calculations. Each member of the alliance was assessed $10,000 to help pay for a high-powered lobbying team that included Shuster's former chief of staff, Ann Eppard, and a former professional associate of one of his daughters. The alliance was Shuster's personal army to achieve a career objective. He had long argued that counting the trust funds in the budget, as the federal government has done since 1969, was an accounting fraud intended to make the deficit look smaller. Members of the Budget Committee saw it differently: They regarded Shuster's move as a raw attempt to gain more control over pork-barrel projects. "As soon as you start talking balanced budgets, there are people who want to take everything off budget," said Robert Walker of Pennsylvania, one of Kasich's allies. "It does strike me as something that people kind of expect of Washington politicians."

Each alliance member was assigned to lobby a group of familiar congressional offices and instructed to write and sign daily reports rating the status of lawmakers on the issue: yes, leaning yes, uncommitted, leaning no, and no. In a late blitz, they organized a call-a-thon with a rehearsed script, and kept up the pressure at Leesburg with faxes addressed to individual members and an open warning by Shuster. Taking the floor after Kasich's review of transportation cuts, Shuster, a fastidious dresser with the silver pompadour of a fifties-era crooner, looked directly at the budget chairman. "John,

I want to make it as clear as I can from the beginning. When I talk about multibillion cuts in my committee, it is predicated on our ability to take the trust funds out of the general budget. I don't know if I can muster the votes among my committee members [otherwise]. You're asking us to walk the plank."

While Shuster's bid gained in Congress, with more than 205 sponsors, it was largely ignored by Kasich and his Budget Committee colleagues when they returned to Washington. Running out of time, the lobbying alliance had contractors take a new approach: Ask co-sponsors to tell party whips testing support for the budget bill that they were undecided because of the trust fund issue. The leadership called Shuster's bluff, and turned back his efforts to force the issue before the budget reached the floor. But Speaker Gingrich, who had served on Shuster's committee, did not want to leave him upset. "Shuster is my problem, I'll deal with him," he told Kasich.

Late on the afternoon before the budget vote, Gingrich called Shuster into his office, declared himself a "pro-infrastructure Republican," and promised to help resolve the trust fund issue after the budget passed. The next day, as Shuster was voting for the budget, Gingrich released a letter announcing the formation of a Speaker's Task Force on Transportation with Kasich, Shuster, and Appropriations Committee Chairman Bob Livingston, who also had opposed Shuster's power play. The task force would be headed by Gingrich and would attempt to "develop a consensus on the issue."

Shuster declared victory. He and his Road Gang voted for the budget.

Gingrich also played the central role in resolving the Aggie revolt. After persuading Kasich to lop a few billion off his proposed farm cuts at Leesburg, Roberts returned to Washington thinking that even the $9 billion number in farm subsidy savings was too much. On Friday, May 12, he brought forty-one members of his posse into a meeting with Gingrich, away from Kasich and Majority Leader Armey, who was regarded, as one Aggie put it, as "the Darth Vader of rural America" because of his longstanding efforts to eliminate farm subsidies. Roberts's disdain for Armey was captured during an interview when the majority leader's name was mentioned. "What was the name?" Roberts asked coolly.

Roberts first tried the economic argument on Gingrich. He cited lenders who questioned the creditworthiness of farmers in a subsidy-free market and conveyed the threat of steeply declining land values depicted in a Kansas State University study. The "K State Report," as it became known, stunned Republican leaders with its predictions of a 50 percent drop in Kansas land values if farm programs were eliminated. Then Roberts and his Aggie allies repeated to Gingrich the political costs of allowing the Democrats to frame the budget as a war on rural America. "These are our people," Roberts told the speaker, evoking the deep rural pockets of Republicanism which, along with votes on election day, helped fill the GOP coffers: the agriculture sector contributed $1.5 million to Republicans in the first six months of their reign.

Gingrich, the history professor, recalled Truman's sweep of the farm vote in 1948 and the Republican shellacking in 1958 after Ike's agriculture secretary tried to end the farm subsidies, as well as the political troubles caused by the farm recession of the mid-1980s. "We have to be careful it doesn't happen again," the speaker concluded. He already had intervened on behalf of the Aggies once earlier, when Roberts had pleaded for the life of food stamps. This $27 billion program was supposed to be replaced by direct cash payments to the states, a plan drawn from the Contract with America and supported by half the House leadership. Gingrich was persuaded that the move would taint Republicans as the "anti-rural party." He overruled Armey's antisubsidy faction in that case, and ordered that the program be left alone.

But Gingrich now appreciated Kasich's need to keep the cuts at $9 billion, so he and Roberts devised an extraordinary fail-safe provision in the budget resolution to protect the Aggies. Most of the farm subsidy cuts had been deferred to the last two years. Language was written into the bill instructing Congress to reexamine the planned cuts for those years unless there were a number of favorable farm developments: steady land values, tax and regulatory relief, and free trade unencumbered by subsidies for foreign competitors. As a final sweetener, Gingrich wrote a letter to Roberts promising in the inevitable House-Senate conference committee to "closely consider" the Senate's plan, which was more advantageous to farmers. Roberts and the Aggies voted unanimously for Kasich's budget.

Kasich's colleagues, especially Gingrich, kept warning him that his mission after that first victory—getting a balanced budget all the way through Congress and past President Clinton—would be infinitely harder than anything he had yet attempted. When Republicans were in the minority and were presenting alternative budgets that had no chance of passage, all they needed was a strong kayak to shoot the rapids of public opinion, Gingrich warned Kasich in a memo. Now they would need something more durable, a steel-plated submarine that could survive the incessant attacks sure to come from the Democrats.

Kasich did not consider this a mission impossible. He knew all along how hard it would be. He knew there would be "no brass bands playing at the end." But it reminded him of his boyhood days at the ball yard behind Fenton School. "We got up there at nine in the morning, and we'd have eighteen guys show up and we played baseball all day, and when we would get done, you would be so dry, you go to the garden hose, and that water would touch your mouth and it was a little bit of heaven. Back then we were all very enthusiastic about playing. We played hard. We played fair. And as a smaller guy, I had to give it everything. And that's where my arguing came from, never giving up on an argument. Because let me tell you, when you thought the ball was out, and they thought the ball was fair, and this was the bottom of the last inning and you're gonna lose the game, and you've been playing this game for hours, you don't give in."

FIVE

Revenge of the Business Class

IN HIS ROLES as small-town industrialist, civic benefactor, and veteran congressman from the western hills of North Carolina, Thomas Cass Ballenger always displayed a talent for raising money. But the fund-raising never came easier than during the congressional elections of 1994, when he traveled around his state soliciting contributions for candidates who would serve as ground troops for the Republican Revolution. Wherever Ballenger spoke, checkbooks opened at the mention of the Occupational Safety and Health Administration, a regulatory agency that had emerged as a symbol of everything the business world disliked about the federal government. His vision of a House of Representatives controlled by Republicans, as Ballenger later described it, went like this:

"I'd say, 'Guess who might be chairman of the committee who'd be in charge of OSHA?'

"And they'd say, 'Who?'

"And I'd say, 'Me!'

"And I'd say, 'I need some money.' And—whoosh!—I got it. This was my sales pitch: 'Businessmen, wouldn't you like to have a friend overseeing OSHA?' "

Indeed they would.

They liked the idea so much that they immediately gave Ballenger more than $65,000 to distribute to Republican candidates, including five from North Carolina who went on to win seats previously held by Democrats. The partisan transformation of the Tarheel delegation was an essential part of the Republican takeover of the House, and it led, among other things, to a new and decidedly pro-management chairman for the House subcommittee on workforce protections: Cass Ballenger. A panel that for years had been controlled by the son of a Michigan auto worker killed in an industrial fire was now headed by a deceptively easygoing, sixty-eight-year-old good ole boy from Hickory who was educated at Amherst, inherited his family's box company, and made his fortune producing plastic bags for underwear.

Ballenger and his allies swiftly moved to make good on their campaign promise. With the strong support of business coalitions, including corporations that were both repeated OSHA violators and leading financial contributors to the Republican Party, they pushed the most concerted legislative effort to diminish the agency's powers since its creation a quarter century ago, moving to shrink the size of the investigative staff, shift the emphasis to consultation, eliminate independent research and mine safety operations, and curtail OSHA's powers to penalize workplaces that fail to meet federal health and safety standards. The attempt to refashion the safety and health agency, in combination with efforts to repeal wage and union security laws enacted over decades by Congress's old Democratic majority, amounted to what labor scholars called the most serious effort to rewrite the rules of the American workplace in favor of business interests in the postwar era.

It also was a serious effort to weaken organized labor and weaken a cornerstone of the Democratic coalition. Laws passed in the Depression years that protected the right of workers to bargain collectively, earn minimum wages, and go on strike without fear of replacement led to the dramatic growth of unions—and to their commitment to reelect Democratic allies. Although in recent decades unions had declined significantly in membership and voting power by the time Gingrich and his troops arrived, incoming Republican leaders saw an opportunity to deliver what labor economist Harley Shaiken called "one final onslaught against the remaining power that labor has." But instead of dealing a final blow, the anti-OSHA effort backfired on the Republicans. Unions became revitalized by the threat, and later helped Democrats block initiatives that were even more central to the revolution.

In the early days of their power, Republicans insisted on challenging every totem of the old order, including the central question on which the vast federal health and safety system was based: Whom do you trust with a worker's welfare, the employer or a federal regulator? "I think employers now take a different approach with their workers than they have in the past," said Lindsey Graham, a freshman Republican from South Carolina and member of Ballenger's subcommittee. "My job is to get the government up to speed with the times. And the times for me are to reevaluate the role of the federal government in private business. If you believe that is the mandate, OSHA is a great place to start."

Although OSHA was established during the presidency of Richard Nixon and has been run by Republican-appointed administrators for eighteen of its twenty-six years, it was scorned by House Republicans as the archetype of a liberal program gone astray. They described it as a place where swarms of inspectors swooped down to intimidate innocent merchants, professionals, and manufacturers, where bureaucrats drown businesses in paperwork and are more interested in imposing fines than ensuring safety. "They need to do what the hell they're told," was the feeling of Charlie Norwood, a dentist from Georgia and the most intense of the Republican freshmen in his dislike of the agency. "They've been sitting in their little cubicles for twenty-five years thinking they knew what was best for every industry in this country. They don't. And they don't want to know. All they want to know is what they can get away with to collect money from us."

Many Democrats found their position ironic. Year after year they had complained that OSHA was ineffective and needed more inspectors and tougher standards. In the 103rd Congress, before they lost control, Democrats had pushed legislation strengthening the agency in the very places where Republicans later sought to weaken it. But now they were caught in a rearguard action defending the status quo, arguing that the agency, for all its faults, had been a savior for American workers. They cited statistics showing that OSHA saved an estimated six thousand lives each year and led to significant decreases in workplace injuries and illnesses. Behind the cover of reform, they said, Republicans were exacting corporate revenge, using the paperwork complaints of small businesses to enrich the management class at the expense of blue-collar workers.

For years business had felt an obligation to pay homage to the Democratic masters of Congress, even when their interests differed. The Republican takeover created opportunities to bring politics in line with corporate objectives, none more important than rewriting labor laws and loosening the grip of government regulations. Corporations dedicated their lobbying armies to the anti-OSHA campaign, joining a debate that crackled with fiery rhetoric and melodramatic anecdotes. From the business world came a bumper sticker that only slightly exaggerated the prevailing sentiment: "OSHA is America's KGB—It Turns the American Dream into a Nightmare." In the matter-of-fact words of John Boehner of Ohio, a former plastics salesman who became a member of the House Republican leadership and its liaison to business: "Most employers would describe OSHA as the Gestapo of the federal government." Business leaders would pass along tales of bureaucratic overzealousness, such as the case in Augusta, Georgia, where a nonprofit group was fined $7,500 for using mothballs to chase squirrels out of the attic and failing to post a notice describing the chemicals in the mothballs.

From labor came a sarcastic title for Ballenger's effort—the

"Death and Injury Enhancement (DIE) Act." Democrat Major Owens of New York, ranking minority member of the subcommittee, used a congressional hearing to read off the names of men and women killed in the workplace and likened the toll to the death count in Vietnam. Unionists recalled workplace tragedies that might have been avoided if not for management carelessness, such as the case in Grand Island, Nebraska, where a maintenance man at a meat-packing plant had his "head popped like a zit," in the indelicate phrase of a co-worker, when he tried to retrieve his pliers from a carcass-defleshing machine that turned on because it lacked the required safety locks.

CASS Ballenger saw more than a few workplace injuries during his years as a manufacturer in Hickory, an industrial town whose streets are lined with hosiery mills. When he switched his family business from boxes to plastic bags, he often worked the machines himself. A contraption called the scoring machine was particularly troublesome, he said. "The clutch on it was mechanical and the dang thing always slipped. You'd be wiping grease off it and the cloth would get caught in the gears and—*thwack!*—it would just cut your fingers off." That was before the days of OSHA, Ballenger noted, and employers and workers relied on "simple common sense." Ballenger kept all his digits, but when someone at his plant lost a finger, he would say, " 'See what can happen? Put the guard back on and don't do that again.' You learn not to do that anymore."

From the first time inspectors visited his factory, his relationship with government regulators was quarrelsome. "They came into my plant and they told me that my loading dock was unsafe because it didn't have a barrier to keep people from falling off," he recalled. "And so I said, 'Well, let me ask you something, if you put a barrier up, how do you load?' They thought about it and said maybe they were wrong." Ballenger is a southern storyteller who acknowledges that he occasionally delves into hyperbole to make points. Whether the loading-dock inspection happened precisely as Ballenger remembered it is unclear. There are no records of the event. But it is important for two reasons. First, in the business world's catalogue of nonsensical OSHA violations, an assortment that includes a number of utter myths, the loading-dock episode is prominently featured, told and retold in various versions around the country. Second, it shaped Ballenger's perceptions from then on as he dealt as a lawmaker with government regulators.

North Carolina is among two dozen states where federal workplace standards are enforced at the state level, a form of the devolution of power back to the states that is so popular with the Republican revolutionaries, in other instances at least. When Ballenger was in the state legislature in Raleigh, he sat on the committee overseeing OSHA and constantly fought with the state labor commissioner, John Brooks. "Every time John came in and said, 'We are underfunded and need more inspectors,' and told us how it was awful that we didn't think about the health and safety of the workers of North Carolina," Ballenger said, he would be thinking, "Here's this horse's ass who runs a lousy operation asking us for more money."

There was a personal aspect to Ballenger's animosity that extended beyond the loading-dock incident. He accused Brooks of conducting "political raids" on his bag plant, inspecting it three times only because he was a prominent Republican in what was then a Democratic state government. Brooks called the accusation groundless: Factories were chosen for inspection by a random computer system. "There is no human way to tamper with the system," Brooks said. "Cass knows that and was offered the opportunity to see it working."

"If you believe that," Ballenger responded, "I've got a bridge I'd like to sell you."

FROM the time he reached Washington in 1987 as a House freshman, boasting that he was the only member who had been cited for workplace violations, Ballenger worked on OSHA legislation with a group of Republicans on the old Education and Labor Committee. Their efforts were defensive, trying to stop the

Democrats and their labor allies from expanding the agency's powers. "Then all of a sudden, oops! We got control," Ballenger said of the 1994 elections. His first task as chairman of the workforce protections subcommittee was to pick a team of Republican lawmakers to help him dismantle the agency. "I wanted people sympathetic to the cause," he said. "I was looking for pro-business people."

Harris Fawell of suburban Chicago had been working with Ballenger on OSHA bills during the Democratic era and would be helpful this time around. Bill Barrett of Nebraska carried the complaints of the meat-packing plants in his district. Tim Hutchinson of Arkansas, whose district included the chicken giant Tyson Foods, would look out for the poultry processors. Peter Hoekstra of Michigan, who came out of the furniture industry, "hated OSHA with a passion," Ballenger thought. James Greenwood of suburban Philadelphia was the most moderate of the veterans, but Ballenger respected him. "I asked him where he would stand on OSHA," Ballenger recalled. "And he said, 'I'll be with you.' " Then Ballenger recruited three freshmen. He brought in David Funderburk, one of the gang of five from North Carolina. "Oh, I knew Funderburk. Hoo, boy!" said Ballenger, explaining that he considered his Tarheel colleague even more conservative than he was. When Lindsey Graham of South Carolina signed on, Ballenger hailed him as "a good ole southern boy—you can count on them every time." And finally there was Charles Norwood, the dentist from Augusta who arrived in Washington with OSHA dead in his sights. "Everybody knew about Charlie," Ballenger said, smiling.

For all the decades that the labor subcommittees were dominated by Democrats, Republicans willing to be assigned to them tended to be moderates. Now, in the era of Republican rule, Cass Ballenger looked at his group and declared that he was about to have some fun. "My subcommittee is so conservative it makes me look liberal," he said. "We could kill motherhood tomorrow if it was necessary." One of his freshmen put it another way. "This was a subchapter of the AFL-CIO for twenty years," said

Lindsey Graham. "Now everybody here talks slower—and with a twang."

THE lobbyists heard the twang, and took it as their call to action. At three on the afternoon of January 30, 1995, not long after the Republicans assumed control of Congress, some one hundred of the GOP's most powerful allies in the business world gathered in the Washington boardroom of the National Association of Manufacturers. Oil was there, and chemicals, along with freight and construction and steel and small business. They convened as members of a lobbying group known as COSH, the Coalition on Occupational Safety and Health, and they sensed that their time was at hand. "We're in a position to get something for employers," said coalition official Pete Lunnie, opening the meeting. As he spoke, Lunnie was struck by how unusual it all seemed, especially the optimistic tone. For several years, the business community had been on the defensive in Congress. The low point had come on April 8, 1992, when an executive had flown cross-country to testify before the House Education and Labor Committee, only to be ignored by the panel's chairman and never called on during a five-hour hearing. Lunnie sent out a membership memo the next day deriding what he called the "crude affront."

But now there were friends everywhere. Along with Ballenger and his subcommittee boys, two former members of the House labor panel had risen to power in the leadership: Armey, the majority leader, and Boehner, the GOP Conference chairman. John Boehner had been deeply involved in OSHA issues in past years and could be counted on again. But at the strategy session in Washington, Lunnie quickly focused on the most important ally. "Cass wants our input," he said. He asked the participants to identify their industry's most pressing problems with OSHA, a process that lasted ninety minutes. From that catalogue of gripes, Lunnie and his core group of lobbyists produced a consensus list of thirty recommendations for revising the agency. In late February, they typed out the suggestions on a single-spaced piece of paper, which they presented to Chairman Ballenger. When Ballenger's subcommittee came out with the Safety and Health Improvement and Regulatory Reform Act of 1995 in early June, after the House had dealt with its Contract with America, there was little doubt among congressional insiders about who benefited from each section of the forty-seven-page document. Virtually everything on COSH's wish list was there.

The coalition was the largest of many business groups and lobbyists who found their way to Ballenger's office as the bill was being drafted. "I'd say that any businessman who happened to come up here to see someone in the House would come by my office and say, 'When you draw this thing up, will you look at this, please?' " Ballenger said. "We had several groups that came up with finished bills they wanted. The North Carolina Citizens for Business and Industry, of which I've been a member for thirty years, came up with a complete bill. COSH had ideas. We had ex-heads of OSHA come in here and give us advice. They all knew exactly what I should do."

The work of revising OSHA and rewriting American labor laws had already begun in Ballenger's shop even before the heavy lobbying started. Weeks before the 1994 congressional elections, James M. Eagan III, who was then the ranking minority aide on the Education and Labor Committee, had a hunch that the Republicans might gain control of the House and began organizing a plan of action. The staff drafted a document called "Agenda 104," named for the 104th Congress. It outlined the issues facing the committee and identified those of highest priority. Labor laws and OSHA topped the list. When Ballenger assumed control of the subcommittee, he delved deeply into the drafting process, choosing among legislative options presented by aides in daily briefings along with memos from corporate backers. Some industry lobbyists were brought in to press a point or explain its ramifications. Some were enlisted to draft specific provisions, others to vet them. While COSH and other groups enjoyed broad access to the process, one lobbyist had the inside track: Dorothy Livingston Strunk.

A coalminer's daughter from Pennsylvania who arrived in

Washington with a high school diploma, Dotty Strunk had undergone a long rise through the ranks to emerge as one of the most powerful voices in the workplace safety field. For years she had been a top Republican aide on the Labor Committee. In 1987, President Reagan nominated her to run the Mine Safety and Health Administration (MSHA), but her appointment was killed in the Senate after strong opposition from the United Mine Workers, who called her unqualified. During the Bush administration, she moved over to OSHA, where she rose from deputy to acting director.

Strunk later became a lobbyist for United Parcel Service, a company whose Santa Claus–like public image as the present deliverers covers an intensely political enterprise with a history of workplace difficulties. During the 1994 election cycle, UPS, which is one of the nation's top five employers and has offices in every congressional district, ranked as the nation's number-one PAC contributor, giving more than $2.6 million. Like many major PAC givers, it leaned heavily Republican after the GOP takeover, contributing more than a half million dollars to Republican House members alone—an average of $2,100 per member. For Ballenger and five members of his labor panel, the campaign purse opened wider. Together, they pulled in $30,000 from the delivery service.

The relationship between UPS and OSHA has been lengthy and costly. The agency has received more worker complaints against UPS than any other employer, resulting since 1972 in 2,786 violations and $4.6 million in fines. The company insists that most of the cases were minor. But according to data it supplied to the Teamsters Union, UPS workers suffered 10,555 lifting and lowering injuries that required more than first aid in 1992. As another measure of its safety record, the firm pays out more than $1 million a day in workmen's compensation.

UPS had an intense interest in loosening OSHA controls, particularly those dealing with cumulative stress disorders from repetitive motion or lifting. More than 180,000 of its workers perform such tasks, driving the boxy brown UPS trucks or handling packages. In Strunk, they had a lobbyist who not only knew OSHA regulations inside out but also had unusual access to the committee where she had once worked. During the period when the bill was being drafted, it was not uncommon for aides to other congressmen to enter the committee offices and see Strunk emerging from a back-room meeting with Gary L. Visscher, the staffer assigned to writing the OSHA bill. When the first version of the legislation made the rounds in April, it was often referred to as "Dotty's draft."

Her influence was clear in Ballenger's bill. Strunk and other lobbyists from the construction and trucking industries wanted to blunt the only tool OSHA had to prevent cumulative trauma disorders such as carpal tunnel syndrome and back strain. The agency had been struggling for years to issue an ergonomics standard that would cover those health problems, but in the meantime invoked a general duties clause in its statute to deal with "recognized hazards" of the workplace that were not specially addressed. The general duty clause is used against a wide range of otherwise unregulated risks. Starting in the 1980s, it became a popular OSHA tool to prevent cumulative trauma disorders. By 1990, eight hundred ergonomic violations were imposed by OSHA — one-quarter of its general duty clause cases — costing employers more than $3 million in fines. Four UPS facilities were among those cited for package sorting and loading practices. Facing $140,000 in fines, the company contested the charges, arguing that because there were no specific ergonomic standards, it should not be accused of failing to meet them. OSHA backed off for lack of sufficient evidence.

The Ballenger bill offered an opportunity for corporations to achieve what had eluded them for a quarter century. His staff presented a number of options to narrow the general duty clause, adding language to limit its application. Then, at a crucial meeting in the chairman's office, Strunk presented a historical perspective that turned the discussion in favor of her client. The original drafters, she noted, wanted the clause to be used sparingly, but enforcers over the years stretched the provision to apply it more liberally. No restrictions, she implied, would hold for long.

Ballenger was in no mood to take chances. His bill effectively eliminated the general duty clause by preventing OSHA from imposing penalties where no specific standard exists. While the bill solved one problem for UPS, it might have created a bigger one at any other time. Without the general duty powers, pressure for specific standards to deal with the fastest-growing injury would be expected to increase. Half of today's workforce uses computers, requiring repetitive motion similar to that of slaughterhouse workers cutting meat and grocery store clerks using price scanners. OSHA was getting ready to unveil its ergonomics plans early in 1995.

But in the antiregulatory mood of 1995, Strunk easily headed off the plans. Toting a 628-page OSHA draft that she called "Ergo Light," she successfully lobbied House appropriators to cut off funds for issuing ergonomics standards. The freeze bought time for the Ballenger bill, which made it highly unlikely that new standards could be imposed in the future. The measure would require extensive analyses to justify the costs of a new rule to any industry, a long and complicated process. In addition, Ballenger was persuaded by Ashland Oil to have such justifications reviewed by panels of experts, including those from companies with potential interest in the outcome.

THE Ballenger effort was pro-business in its contours, turning a feared regulatory agency into what amounted to a consultant to employers. It would funnel half the budget into training programs and incentives for voluntary action. Large numbers of employers were exempted from random inspections and given more chances to avoid penalties, while the rights of workers to file OSHA complaints were diminished. As in the case of UPS and ergonomics, the fine print of the bill showed the influence of many industries. Chemical companies reached one of their longtime goals by keeping states from exceeding OSHA standards on workplace safety, such as the labeling of toxic substances. Another provision, inspired by Dow Chemical Company, would free employers regulated by OSHA from other federal rules that were "potentially in conflict." Pushed by workplace subcommittee member Peter Hoekstra of Michigan, whose congressional district is close to Dow's headquarters in Midland, the provision was supposed to prevent double regulation. But critics saw it as a way for industry to bypass the tougher rules of other agencies if they could be shown to be remotely similar to those of OSHA.

The iron and steel lobby persuaded Ballenger to drop a requirement that records be kept for work-related illnesses, such as hearing loss, that do not result in medical treatment or lost time. OSHA uses such logs to target troubled industries for inspection, a practice particularly threatening to the noisy primary metals industry, because OSHA was planning to tighten standards for hearing loss. The number of reported cases was almost certain to rise and draw the scrutiny of OSHA inspectors—unless the record-keeping requirement was waived.

One of the most sweeping of Ballenger's proposals would abolish the federal agency charged with mine safety and transfer its reduced regulatory powers to a weakened OSHA. The Mine Safety and Health Administration was regarded as a regulatory success story, bringing about a sevenfold drop in mine fatalities since 1968. Ballenger's bill gave it weaker enforcement powers against unsafe mines and looser training and inspection requirements. Instead of four inspections per year, underground mines would face one. The requirement for two surface mine inspections a year was dropped. Ballenger explained the decision as a budget-driven effort to save money and streamline federal authority. But larger economic constituencies loomed in the background. The most influential background adviser advocating the merger was Dotty Strunk, who after leaving government worked for a law firm that represented mining interests.

The proposal was supported by owners and operators of the rich East Kentucky coal fields, whose small mines are among the most dangerous and the latest targets of MSHA. And in the northeast corner of Ballenger's district, Mitchell County is the nation's largest producer of feldspar, a sandlike mineral mined on the surface and used in ceramic and glass products. Ballenger met with an official of one of the mining outfits there: "He said what really bugged him was, being above ground and so forth, he gets inspected by both OSHA and MSHA. So he's got two sets of rules to work off."

WHILE there was basic agreement among subcommittee members and industry allies about the scope of the OSHA bill, there were some moments of tension. Freshman Charlie Norwood, the dentist from Augusta, thought the bill seemed too timid, tinkering with the system instead of remaking it. Several lobbyists shared his view. In May, a few weeks before the measure was presented, Norwood and his freshmen compatriots requested a meeting with Ballenger. They asked John Boehner from the leadership to help them make their case.

Boehner had spent much of the past four years working on OSHA revisions that went nowhere because of the previous Democratic majorities. He generally agreed with Norwood that staffers drafting the bill with Strunk's assistance "seemed to be too locked in on what is instead of developing a completely new vision of what could be." On the other hand, he had heard about Norwood's sentiment to just close OSHA down entirely, and realized that was not politically possible. When the meeting began, Boehner said, he was more on the side of Norwood and the freshmen. But soon enough he found himself aligning with Ballenger, explaining to Norwood why certain things could not be done.

"Charlie wanted to prevent OSHA from entering the workplace where there was a serious accident or death if the employer's lost-work ratio was below the industry average," Boehner recalled. "It was one of those issues where you had to walk Charlie through the politics of it, the practicality of it. The politics of it are: 'Charlie, how do you defend that?' If you're going to have OSHA and your goal is to create greater safety in the workplace and somebody dies in the workplace, you have to let them in."

Norwood had been taking aim at OSHA since the day he announced for Congress early in 1994, calling himself a dentist and small business man "who just got pushed too far" by government regulators. It had started for him a decade earlier, when OSHA began taking an active role in the dental profession to ensure that employees and patients were not endangered by bloodborne pathogens such as the AIDS virus. Dentists, Norwood said, did not need to be inspected to maintain safe offices. He became so upset by the federal health and safety standards, which he said required his dental team to use two hundred pairs of gloves each day and set up laundry services within his office, that he began placing an explicit "OSHA surcharge" on the bills he sent to patients. The charges amounted to about $10 per visit. When patients complained, Norwood told them to call their congressman.

Then he decided he wanted to be the congressman. Although he had never run for political office, he had developed a state and national political network of dentists from his earlier position as president of the Georgia Dental Association. Much like Ballenger in North Carolina, Norwood had been motivated in part by personal experience. The Department of Labor had once investigated him for not paying overtime to his office aides after a disgruntled former employee filed a complaint. Norwood said it would have cost him more to fight the complaint than settle it, but he never forgot the $10,000 incident. From then on, he referred to federal investigators as "storm troopers."

One morning on the campaign trail, he turned to a young aide and asked him to find out who was in charge of OSHA. The assistant called Washington and learned that it was an undersecretary of labor named Joseph Dear. From then on, whenever he spoke to businessmen in his district, Norwood would say, "You know, that fellow Joe Dear, well, when I get up to Washington I'm gonna call that Joe Dear at five every morning and explain to him the problems at OSHA." He never followed through on that campaign vow, but he did invite Dear to meet with him in his congressional office. Norwood complained that the bloodborne pathogen standards were so strict that dentists felt they could not give children their extracted teeth. It was a story that Norwood and other dentists had been telling for years, so common that it even had a name—The Tooth Fairy Story—and like so many of the OSHA "horror stories," as they are called, it fell somewhere between reality and myth, but closer to myth. Some dentists did stop giving out teeth, but there was nothing in the law that prevented them from doing so.

Norwood also asked Dear about another common story—that OSHA regulations prohibited roofers from chewing gum on the job. Dear said there was no such regulation. Norwood later claimed that he had caught Dear in a lie. Again, the anti-OSHA troops were weaving a thread of reality into a fabric of myth: OSHA standards did say workers should not chew gum in one case—when they were working "in an area where the level of asbestos is so high that chewing could result in the ingestion of asbestos."

While Norwood and other Republicans on the subcommittee relied on their catalogue of horror stories to make their case against OSHA, the struggle had a strong economic and political component to it as well. PAC contributions from corporations lobbying on OSHA and other labor laws dominated Norwood's list of donors since his election. Two-thirds of the money he raised to retire his campaign debt came from members of those lobbying coalitions. More than half of the $230,000 he raised from PACs for his next election came from those same groups, boosting him to fourth place among freshman recipients of PAC money. Dentists, who played an active role in the anti-OSHA movement, contributed more than $90,000 to his last campaign. In return, Norwood essentially made dentists exempt from OSHA safety inspections: they fell into the category of small businesses that would no longer be visited by the green and yellow–jacketed OSHA investigators. Dentists gave thanks: $45,000 in contributions to Norwood in his first year in office.

Subcommittee member Bill Barrett's largest source of money was from the meat, poultry, and sugar interests, all of which were pushing to relax OSHA controls of their industries. His largest contributions in 1994 and for 1996, totaling $11,800, came from ConAgra, the agribusiness giant, which also accounted for the largest OSHA violations in his district in the past five years. ConAgra's mammoth Monfort meat-packing plant in Grand Island was hit with fines of over $625,000 after a series of incidents there, including the death of a maintenance man who was beheaded by a machine that should have had a safety lock.

More than one-third of the PAC money raised by Chairman Ballenger in 1994 came from corporations that were lobbying for OSHA changes. When he took the chairman's seat in 1995, the ratio jumped to 70 percent. The most generous donor both years was UPS's PAC, giving a total of $15,000. The single largest contribution he solicited for the National Republican Congressional Committee was from Glaxo Inc., a major North Carolina chemical firm that had a long history of working in tandem with Ballenger to fight OSHA. When Ballenger was in the North Carolina legislature, Glaxo was fighting a revision in the law that would have required it to have a locked mailbox at the plant gate that contained all of the reports on chemicals shipped into the plant each day. "You had to change it every day if you received chemical shipments every day," Ballenger recalled. The company considered it a paperwork headache. "Luckily," said Ballenger, "I killed the hell out of it."

THE complaint from labor and Democrats for years was that OSHA was doing too little. Of the seventy thousand hazardous chemicals used by industry, the agency had set standards for only twenty-five, an average of one each year. It had only in the last two years begun moving seriously on ergonomics—a regulation that employers fear above all others, and that several unions see as their rallying cry for the next generation. Its inspections were few and far between. In different states, the average company might be inspected once every seven to twenty-three years. In the aftermath of the most calamitous workplace disaster of the 1990s, the September 3, 1991, fire at Imperial Food Products in Hamlet, North Carolina, where twenty-five people died because there was no sprinkler system and the fire doors could not be opened from the inside, it was discovered that OSHA had never inspected the plant.

There were significant gains in some areas, however, which strengthened the resolve of OSHA supporters as they fought for the agency's life. The impact of regulatory intervention in certain high-risk industries is clear. There have been 58 percent fewer deaths in grain handling and 35 percent fewer deaths in trench cave-ins since OSHA cracked down on those industries. The number of textile workers suffering from brown lung—a crippling respiratory disease—fell from 20 percent of the industry workforce in 1978, when OSHA set limits on worker exposure to cotton dust, to 1 percent seven years later. Democrat Major Owens of New York said that the Republican attempts to change the American workplace amounted to a declaration of war on the nation's working men and women.

But Lindsey Graham said the Democrats and labor were mistaken if they thought they had the working people on their side. Graham, forty-one, grew up in the textile town of Seneca, South Carolina, where his parents ran the Sanitary Cafe, a bar outside the factory gate. It was a beer and hot dog place with a jukebox that played "Satin sheets to lie on, satin pillows to cry on." When the factory shift changed at three every afternoon, young Graham would see mill workers "come in with their shirts covered with cotton, white as they could be. There'd be a finger missing on every other person." Although he considered his hometown an "Andy Griffith of Mayberry–type place," Graham also saw the failings of the old system. The textile plant treated its workers like children, he said, and placed a greater emphasis on productivity than safety.

Graham understood that it was necessary for the government to intercede and make workplaces safer, just as he realized that the segregated system his parents were part of—they made black workers buy beer from a takeout window out back—was wrong and required the force of government action to eradicate. But by the time Graham ran for Congress in 1994, he had been convinced that the pendulum had swung too far toward federal intervention. He thought the role of the government in mandating affirmative action and regulating workplaces had "gone from being helpful to being the biggest obstacle dividing and polarizing the nation by race and by employers and employees."

It was his generation's mission, Graham said, to "correct the excesses of government from the past generation."

One day during his congressional race, Graham had what his campaign manager, David Woodard, called "an epiphany." Graham had delivered a noon speech at a small-town Rotary Club, where he received a tepid response. Concerned that he had not figured out how to tap into the old southern Democratic establishment, Graham then paid a visit to a textile mill on the edge of town. He later told Woodard that the plant manager was so agitated he threw a sheaf of papers to the ground and bellowed, "No more damn Democrats! They've got all these inspectors on me. All these crappy regs!" Afterward, Graham placed an excited call to his campaign manager. "We may not have the Rotary, but we have the people running the mills," he said. And maybe the people working the mills. From then on, he picked up the theme of government deregulation, a message that helped him become the first Republican elected in his district since Reconstruction.

He brought the message to Washington and let it resonate one spring day at a subcommittee hearing as he listened to the testimony of Labor Secretary Robert Reich, the Harvard professor who for years has advised Democrats on the declining competitiveness of American workers. Graham, who won 60 percent of the vote in a district where the average income was $13,200, said he counted the times Reich used the phrase "working stiff" in his presentation. The labor secretary uttered those words twenty-one times. "Working stiff?" Graham thought to himself. "The working stiffs elected me." They chose him over the Democrats. He asked Reich one question: "How do you reconcile your agenda with my election?"

SIX

Dick Armey's Big Boot

WHILE NEWT GINGRICH spent much of his time sequestered in his second-floor office plotting strategy for the next war, the daily assault on the federal government was being directed from the floor above his in the office of the House majority leader. Gingrich was the undisputed leader of the revolution, but the troops were Armey's army. It was Dick Armey, a slow-motion Texas hulk in cowboy boots, who scheduled what the Republicans did every day on the House floor, and it was largely his sober demeanor and free market resolve that drove the agenda.

To Armey, dismantling the federal bureaucracy (or the expansionist welfare state, in the lexicon of the revolution) was an academic, ideological, and personal quest. He disdained government both in theory and practice with an intensity that grew over the years even as government paid his bills, first as professor and then as lawmaker. In that sense it could be said that Armey was the quintessential conservative contradiction: someone drawn to government out of distaste for government. Like Gingrich, his animus seemed motivated in part by his tribulations in the liberal realm of academia. He had surpassed the speaker there in one respect at least, gaining tenure, but that had given him little comfort on campus. During the early days of the Reagan era, when heady conservatives were first calling themselves revolutionaries, Armey toiled in distant obscurity as an economics professor at North Texas State University in Denton. He was a self-described "bush league professor at a bush league school," squabbling incessantly with colleagues who considered him a power-grabbing lightweight and wanted to dump him as department chairman.

From those days through his rise to the position of majority leader, Armey's ideology changed very little. His reputation occasionally veered in surprising directions, but it always came back to his mission to unburden capitalism from government interference. He was the legislative godfather of the flat tax concept that propelled the presidential candidacy of Steve Forbes. He was the scourge of the minimum wage. He was the nonpartisan innovator who devised a way to close obsolete military bases and joined forces with urban Democrats to attack federal farm subsidies. He was the acerbic ideologue who dismissed President Clinton as "your president" during a debate with Democrats and faced down First Lady Hillary Rodham Clinton with the rejoinder, "The reports on your charm are overstated and the reports on your wit are understated." He was the precise academic who grasped the details of the GOP economic plan. And he was the sloppy speaker who tripped over his tongue, or his subconscious, when he uttered the infelicitous phrase "Barney Fag" in referring to Democrat Barney Frank of Massachusetts.

There is little subtlety to Dick Armey. He speaks in a reverberating bass voice that sounds like he is mixing cement deep inside his throat. His favorite restaurant is Denny's. Susan Armey, the woman who would become his second wife, canceled the wedding on him three times, yet he refused to disappear until he finally got her to say, "I do." His first political mentor was Eddie Chiles, the irascible, right-wing Texas oilman whose slogan was "I'm Eddie Chiles and I'm Still Mad!" When his faculty enemies at North Texas finally got the best of him, Armey resigned by walking into the dean's office and blasting out a rendition of "Take This

Job and Shove It!" on his tape recorder. Not long after he arrived in Washington in 1985, he decided that his apartment in Crystal City was not worth the expense, so he slept on a cot in the House gym until the Democratic leadership unceremoniously evicted him one night and he crashed in his office on the fifth floor of the Cannon House Office Building.

Armey sees no mystery in the dark science of economics. He is a true believer in the free market. Adam Smith and Milton Friedman are his heroes. His proudest moment as a scholar came when Friedman wrote an article in *Newsweek* asking readers to suggest the best phrase describing the harm caused by well-intentioned federal programs. From Denton came Professor Armey's letter nominating "The Invisible Foot of Government." Later, when Friedman's envelope from the University of Chicago arrived declaring Armey the winner of the contest, he was so excited that "it was like, someone please open this letter for me."

Most of his House Republican colleagues appreciated Armey's directness and cited his straightforward manner as one reason he rose from the academic backwaters to national party leadership in one decade. "Dick does not connive, does not conspire, does not manipulate," said Lamar Smith, one of his Republican comrades from Texas. But Democrats were often affronted by his blunt nature. At a leadership meeting at the White House in February 1993, after President Clinton had delivered his first budget, Armey shocked everyone there by launching into a harsh lecture during which he told Clinton that he had based his budget on inaccurate data and the wrong economic model and that his policies would make him a one-term president. This prompted a reproach from Senator Robert Byrd of West Virginia, who quoted "at least three Greek philosophers" in a rebuttal that Armey described as "the finest scolding I've ever had in my life."

For all his plain speaking, however, there are touches of calculation and hyperbole in the Armey persona. He is known on Capitol Hill as a country boy who loves nothing more than to go cat-fishing along the Potomac. Yet his son Scott said that while Armey does fish these days, "the whole time we were growing up, he didn't fish." For years, profiles of Armey featured the story that he decided to run for Congress one night as he was watching the House on C-SPAN, proclaiming to his wife that, shucks, he could do better than that. In fact, Armey confessed, the story was a "joke," and his wife was "always scared people would believe it." The truth was that although the 1984 race was his first, he had been moving toward a political career for years as he grew frustrated in academia.

Then there was the story of Charlie the janitor, a minidrama that Armey invariably included in speeches as his anecdotal attack on bleeding-heart government programs, specifically attempts to increase the minimum wage. As Armey recalled the story, Charlie was a slightly retarded man who swept floors on the night shift at Wooten Hall for nominal pay. Charlie "loved his job," according to Armey, and was in turn loved by the professors who worked in the building. Then, one day in 1977, shortly after the federal government raised the minimum wage, Charlie disappeared. A few months later, Armey encountered him at a grocery store, with his wife and infant child, buying provisions with food stamps. The invisible foot of government had cost Charlie his job, Armey said, "and my heart's been broken about it ever since."

It is an effective story, but Armey is alone in remembering it that way. Four professors who worked at Wooten Hall during that era—Jerry Yeric, Bill Dugger, Hugh Garrett, and Jim Danielson—said they could not recall a janitor named Charlie. Alfred Hurley, chancellor of what is now the University of North Texas, said of Armey's account: "I'm not sure what he meant by that. Janitors at the school are state employees . . . the minimum wage is not applicable in their case."

When told that some former colleagues were uncertain about his version of the Charlie anecdote, Armey said: "People at the university didn't get it. It's not unusual for professors not to get it."

There is a second chapter to the Charlie story that is equally revealing about Armey's habit of using anecdotes to sustain his antigovernment theories. After Charlie left, he said, "the building was unswept and unclean. There was a young man, a young black man, who sat at a couch. Well, not a couch but a kind of bench we had there, with what my kids would call a boom box, turned up too loud. And basically he just sat there and played that thing. So I'll admit I was angry. I called around to find out what the deal was. And the irony of it was, the young man was in a federal jobs training program. And they could afford to have him on the payroll, as it were, because of federal funds, but they didn't train him to turn off the loud music, sweep, and be cordial." Universities and governments operated on the same theory, Armey concluded: "Find the most impossible way to get the job done and then focus all your energies on that."

IN each of his many parts, Dick Armey seems to inspire the same question: Where is this guy coming from? The first and most revealing answer is geographic and cultural, and it turns out to have nothing to do with the 26th congressional district that he has represented for a decade on the rich suburban rim of what is known as the Dallas–Fort Worth Metroplex. Where he is coming from is a place called Cando, pronounced in the affirmative, as in "can do," a lonely little town of fifteen hundred residents on the northern plain of North Dakota. They called him "Dickie" in Cando. He was born there in 1940, one of nine children of Glenn and Mary Armey. No one on either side of the family had ever gone to college. His dad was a high school dropout who rose from FDR's Civilian Conservation Corps to a job removing snow with a scoop shovel, then became manager of the Cando Mill and Elevator, and eventually took ownership of the grain elevator. Dickie's mother, who stood five foot eight and weighed more than 250 pounds, had "the heart of an elephant," her son recalled, and went from picking potatoes to working a grocery store cash register to keeping the books at the grain elevator. Her family was German; her maiden name was Gutslag, which translates as "Good Punch."

The duality of Majority Leader Armey—a somber-looking man who loves to joke and jive, a longtime critic of government who has drawn a paycheck from the taxpayers for most of his career—becomes clear when considering his parents. His father, Armey said, was a serious man who "always worried about, oh, what would people say," and who had a sense of community responsibility that led him to serve as Cando's mayor. Armey's mother was the opposite. Her son called her the Queen of Irreverence. "There was nobody that was a big enough shot to impress her," he said. "She had no use at all for the government." Her favorite expression of disaffection was, "Oh, they think the government owes them a living!"

His early life in Cando also goes a long way toward explaining Armey's economic philosophy. After his father took control of the grain elevator, the family held a daily ritual of the free market. On weekdays at noon, they would all gather around the kitchen table for lunch. "But at one o'clock the whole house had to be quiet because the market reports were coming on. My mother and father would listen to the market reports. Minneapolis grain. They would make decisions, buy or sell, constantly. That was my most profound understanding that the market really works."

But while the Cando grain operation showed Armey the efficiency of free market capitalism, there was also, eventually, a tragic side to it. One day in 1973, Glenn Armey stood inside his elevator, pointed a shotgun at his head, and killed himself. One of his daughters said he was distraught about the financial condition of his business. Dick Armey came home for the funeral and never talked about it again.

THE academic life was never peaceful for Armey. When he went off to Jamestown College, his family scoffed, saying no Armey would make it in higher education. In graduate school at Oklahoma, he was scorned by Keynesians who thought he was irrelevant. There was one shining moment, the summer of 1969, when he took a break from teaching at Austin College to study at the University of Chicago amid the conservative luminaries there—"My first real exposure to the discipline of economics," he would call it. Colleagues said he came back a different man, more political and sure of his convictions.

At his next stop, North Texas State, Armey wrote a controversial paper arguing that housewives were overvalued ("A Realistic View of the Relative Income Shares of Male and Female Homemakers"). A few years into his tenure, he got caught up in a bitter departmental struggle when the economics chairman retired and Armey sought his post. He won the election with the support of several liberal professors who claimed that Armey had made an agreement with them that the chairmanship would rotate every few years. Once Armey took over, the others said, he ran the department like an autocrat and reneged on his promise to share power.

"He showed no interest in rotating the chair," said Bill Dugger, now a professor at the University of Tulsa. "That offended me deeply. He is in favor of term limits for others, but not for himself." That is not to say that everyone in the department who disagreed politically with Armey disliked him or found him despotic. Some of his best friends were liberals, and one young graduate student, Miles Groves, who considered himself "a leftist or Marxist," said Armey backed him when he made controversial statements in the classroom.

Armey said the only reason he took the chairmanship was that the dean asked him to, and that he served at his boss's pleasure, staying on for several years even after a majority of his departmental colleagues began demanding his resignation. It was only when the dean left in 1983, and was replaced by an administrator who was less taken with Armey, that he finally resigned. By then, he was easing into a new life in politics being prepared for him by his behind-the-scenes benefactor, Eddie Chiles, who was a member of the school's board of regents. Chiles, then owner of the Texas Rangers baseball club and a prominent Republican financier, discovered Armey one day after he had inquired of a university vice president whether the institution had "anything like a free market economist." Chiles invited Armey to lunch at the Ranchman's, a steakhouse in the nearby town of Ponder, and struck up a fast friendship. In 1983, when Armey was beginning his race for Congress against a popular Democratic incumbent, Chiles set up his campaign.

The professor began the race with what he joked was "two percent name recognition and a five percent margin of error." No one thought he could win. He was nothing if not an irreverent conservative, his mother's son. He called the Social Security system "a bad retirement program" and a "rotten trick" on the taxpayers. He branded universities "bureaucratic mills." He said the minimum wage should be abolished. He knocked on doors four hours a day for six months—and ended up in Washington.

DURING his early years on Capitol Hill, Armey seemed almost Texas quaint. He refused to bring a tuxedo up from Denton, and kept his family back there, too, commuting from Dallas–Fort Worth to National Airport Tuesday mornings and returning Thursday nights. He wore cowboy boots with his suits. He was beloved by his staff, who found him innovative and willing to delegate assignments. Five members of the original staff still worked for him in 1995. Year by year he gained more clout, devising the military base-closing commission, pushing for tax cuts, explaining his economic theories in plain language that his Republican colleagues could understand. But more than anything else, he wanted to be a player, and it was a bitter experience with his own party that inspired him to make his leadership bid. When President Bush was cutting a tax deal with the Democrats in 1990, Armey considered it a grave mistake and kept asking if he could speak to the president. Richard Darman, Bush's top tax strategist, "kept blocking me," Armey said. "Darman kept saying, 'Well, Armey can't deliver any votes.' So I never got in to make my case."

When the House Republicans rebelled, with Newt Gingrich walking out of the negotiations in an effort to blow them up, Armey received less public notice for his role than he deserved. It was Armey, not Gingrich, who had pushed a resolution through the House Republican Conference instructing the leadership to make it clear to Bush that they would not support new taxes.

Armey concluded from that episode that he had to move into the leadership to make his voice heard. In 1993, he made the power move that set him up to be Gingrich's number-two man when and if the Republicans seized the House. With Gingrich's support, he challenged Jerry Lewis of California for chairmanship of the House Republican Conference. Gingrich saw Armey's potential in two ways—either as a constant threat or a great ally. He decided immediately to strike up a new partnership. "We can either integrate Armey in, or he's going to be a permanent contender for influence, because he is too bright, too energetic, too strong a personality," Gingrich told his staff when Armey won the leadership post. Gingrich began inviting Armey to dinner, sometimes alone, sometimes with other close allies. At the end of the first dinner, Armey confessed that conservative collaboration was all new to him. "I've never flown in formation before," he said. "I honestly don't know if I can fly that way or not."

By the summer of 1994, Armey was in formation, answering Gingrich's call to begin crafting the Contract with America, and preparing himself for what others considered an unlikely transfer of real power. That October, before the congressional elections, he was riding in a limousine with Democrat Dick Gephardt of Missouri, then the House majority leader. Gephardt said to him, "Dick, I notice you haven't thrown your hat in the minority whip race. Why not?"

"Well, Dick," said Armey to Gephardt. "I kinda had my eyes on the majority leader spot."

Gephardt thought it was a joke. Armey was serious, and prescient. Less than three months later, he was moving into his new suite of offices on the third floor of the Capitol, directly above Speaker Gingrich. One of his colleagues, Bill McCollum of Florida, was thinking about challenging him for the job, but Armey slyly disposed of that threat: Even before McCollum could float a serious rumor about his intentions, he was flooded with calls from other members of the Florida delegation, who at Armey's behest were urging him to support the big Texan for the post. They were unaware that McCollum was interested.

Previous majority leaders had kept their offices closer to the House floor; but in keeping with their unified leadership concept,

Armey thought it was more important to set up shop as close as possible to the speaker's quarters, so he took space that previously had belonged to the House Administration Committee. It was far removed from the daily commotion, up a dungeonlike narrow spiral staircase, but Armey spent most of his time in and around the House floor in any case. Gingrich was more likely to remain in his ivory tower, while Armey lumbered down for the give and take of the legislative locker room. "He was in there towel-snappin' and razzin' "—as his assistant, Ed Gillespie, put it, using the argot of the jock-and-fratboy culture popular with the young bucks of the conservative movement.

Armey was in his job only a few weeks when he towel-snapped his way into trouble. On January 27, 1995, in an interview with several Capitol Hill radio correspondents, he was asked a question about the financial arrangements for a book he was writing. The query came in the aftermath of Gingrich's controversial book deal. After commentators and Democrats questioned the ethics of that deal, Gingrich relinquished the advance and agreed to collect only royalties. Armey told the radio reporters that he would donate his book proceeds to charity. Gingrich, he said, was better at taking opposition fire.

"Newt's always able to handle a harangue going on around him better than I am," Armey said. "I like peace and quiet. And I don't need to listen to Barney Fag—Barney Frank—haranguing in my ear because I made a few bucks on a book I worked on. I just don't want to listen to it."

At the time of the interview, no one in the room realized that Armey might have said something insulting. It was only later, when the tape was replayed in the press room, that another reporter caught the "Barney Fag" reference. Armey and his aides expressed amazement at first when they were confronted with the tape. Then Armey explained that he had been tongue-tied during the interview, had not had his coffee yet that morning, and had unintentionally mangled two words together—"Frank" and "harangue." People who had been around Armey knew that he had a history of tripping over words. People who had been around Congress knew that Barney Frank, one of three openly gay members of the House, was called several nicknames behind his back by some antigay colleagues. The least tasteful nickname was "Barney Fag." "There are many ways to mispronounce my name," Frank said. "That one is the least common." Another gay congressman, Republican Steve Gunderson of Wisconsin, came to Armey's defense, saying that he believed there was no malicious intent involved.

Whether it was a mangled phrase or a revelation of subconscious thought, Armey had said something that he regretted. He had stuck his pointy-toed Texas-style cowboy boots in his mouth. It was not the last time it would happen to one of the leaders of the House. They were in a year-long rhetorical battle over the role of the federal government, a war of words with the Democrats and the Clinton White House that had profound policy consequences. Yet as so often happens in politics, they kept giving fresh ammunition to the enemy.

ALTHOUGH they share a few common characteristics, it is hard to imagine two men less alike than Newt Gingrich and Dick Armey. Each was a frustrated academic. At a certain point in his life, each decided that he had outgrown his surroundings, turning to a second wife and a second career to renew himself. But once they reached the top together, their differences became more apparent. Armey was the flour to Gingrich's yeast. Where Gingrich concocted ten ideas every day, Armey stayed focused on the one big idea that had consumed his career: removing the invisible foot of government. Where Gingrich at times could seem arrogant and testy, as though only he knew the answers, Armey was more likely to maintain a steady demeanor and place his trust in his staff and colleagues. Although Gingrich was constantly reciting his favorite leadership motto—Listen, Learn, Help, Lead—he could not always repress his urge to lead before doing any of the other three.

Others in the House leadership understood that they owed their lofty positions to Gingrich. It was his sense of possibilities that pushed the Republicans to majority status. But they also felt closer

DICK ARMEY'S BIG BOOT   83

to Armey. They would not talk about it much, but they all felt it. Gingrich knew it, too. From the moment Armey entered the leadership back in 1993, Gingrich had done everything he could to maintain a brotherly relationship with Armey so the others would not feel a need to choose sides. At meetings, he would almost adoringly call Armey "Richard," a name that only his wife used for the everyman Dick. In this coop of Just Us Chickens, there were different varieties of chickens. Armey was a true conservative on both economic and social issues. Gingrich was a breed apart. He might display more provocative conservative rhetoric, but when it came time to set an agenda or negotiate the substance of a bill, his positions were somewhat harder to predict. Where the speaker might end up was determined by strategy and marketing.

The majority leader had less guile, little strategic sense, and the troops knew instinctively where he would be.

These dynamics allowed Armey to establish his own power base in the House, but he rarely used it to challenge the speaker. They disagreed even before the year began over the scope of the Contract with America. Armey wanted to include a social issue to satisfy and energize the Christian Coalition wing of the party. He pushed to attach a school prayer amendment. Gingrich said no. "Al Hunt will go nuts!" he argued, evoking the name of a *Wall Street Journal* writer and television pundit they often cited as the stereotypical establishment liberal. The prayer in school amendment, Gingrich said, would create an unnecessary media storm about how the Republicans were driven by the Christian right. It would detract from the larger revolution.

The pattern grew increasingly apparent. Armey would argue for the pure conservative position—on abortion, eliminating farm subsidies, closing cabinet departments—and Gingrich, calculating the politics of the situation, would maneuver for a less rigid solution. More often than not, Armey deferred. "Speaker trumps Majority Leader," he would say.

SEVEN

"Thank You, God!"

TWO HOURS AFTER midnight on August 4, 1995, the leaders of the House retreated to the third-floor Capitol suite of Majority Leader Dick Armey to celebrate what they viewed as the victorious conclusion of one of the longest nights of their self-styled revolution. Speaker Gingrich arrived tired and emotional, greeted by Armey and his whips, Tom DeLay and Denny Hastert, and several aides. It was time for the boys to relax: neckties undone, feet up, bottles of Sam Adams and Foster's Ale all around, the brew flowing as freely as Professor Gingrich's inevitable stream of historical allusions.

The House had just approved the most controversial spending measure of the year, an appropriations bill that would go further to cut social service programs and balance the budget than any other. Gingrich began the week conceding privately that the Labor–Health and Human Services bill had no better than a one in three chance. Democrats called it mean-spirited because of its significant cuts in education, summer jobs, and workforce protection. But Gingrich was more troubled by a rift between moderate and conservative Republicans, primarily over abortion, the defining issue of evangelical Christian voters who had been so important to the Republican triumph the previous November. Now their champions in Congress and their rivals faced off for the first time all year, and each faction threatened to take the bill down if it did not

get its way. The leadership finally prevailed after Gingrich successfully lobbied recalcitrant moderates at a midnight meeting, while a
flock of anti-abortion conservatives prayed for guidance in a back
room of the Capitol and finally decided to vote with the speaker.

The battle won, Gingrich sipped ale and talked the night away,
a nostalgic general and his high command. Obsessed recently with
Arthur Wellesley, the first Duke of Wellington, he likened the
appropriations triumph to the way the British expeditionary force
maneuvered against the French during the Peninsular War, a campaign in Portugal and Spain in the early 1800s that eventually led
to Wellington's ascendance and Napoleon's abdication.

Gingrich used the words "magical" and "mystical" and "romantic" to describe his feelings about the 232 House Republicans. He
said they had come through the appropriations process together,
despite their differences, because of a shared sense that they were
"at a special place in history and could not fail." The press did not
understand them, he said. Turning to the communications aides in
the room, he declared: "You guys have to tell reporters if they're
going to cover the Republicans now, they need a romantic view of
history." The aides were struck by the dichotomy. On one hand,
they thought how naive it would sound if they went up to the press
gallery and begged for a more romantic perspective. "That's really
gonna fly," thought Eddie Gillespie, Armey's director of communications. Yet he also felt that Gingrich was somehow right. There
was something going on, he agreed, that the press could not quite
fathom.

By four in the morning, the speaker had moved on to football
metaphors. What the Republicans had accomplished, he said, was
like the old Green Bay Packers sweep during the days of Coach
Vince Lombardi: The opposition knows you are going to run at
them, but they cannot stop you. Lombardi, Gingrich said, believed
that the team that doesn't break in the fourth quarter wins. If you
can hold your side together a little longer than the other side, after the strain of battle, you'll win. But now they were more than a
team, he declared. They were "a family."

To many House Democrats, the Republicans seemed more like

a bloodless monolithic force than a family, moving in obedient unison to Gingrich's dictates and Armey's relentless schedule. Veteran Democrat David Obey of Wisconsin complained that Gingrich and Armey had been "running the place like *The Bridge on the River Kwai*" as they pushed their troops to roll back the Great Society by slashing government programs and adopting a corporate agenda curtailing federal regulations of the workplace and the environment.

Inside the revolution, the situation was more fluid, precarious, and unpredictable than it often appeared. After being out of power for more than four decades, House Republicans were constantly facing situations that they had never before encountered. Gingrich, after building his reputation as a hell-raiser for the minority, now had to call on heretofore unseen talents as a negotiator and gentle persuader to keep his family together. During the early months of the session, he often boasted that he was so focused on the big picture that he rarely knew what was being debated on the House floor. But in the final days of the appropriations fight, his presence loomed large as he brought factions up to meet him in his second-floor quarters, moving from room to room like a doctor making rounds.

In one room would be members of "the Lunch Bunch," moderates from the Northeast and Midwest uneasy with the party's fervor on abortion and regulatory issues. Their rivals were members of the Conservative Action Team, composed largely of westerners and southerners. Pressing for the speaker's ear from a third direction were the New Federalists, eager-beaver freshmen budget cutters plus Budget Committee Chairman John Kasich, who described the brash young outfit as "the tip of the revolutionary spear—the Red Guard." On the socially conservative side there were the House Pro-Life Caucus and the Family Caucus of Christians, who prayed and voted together.

If more personal attention was needed during the final hours, Gingrich worked the House floor himself in a friendly bear-paw-around-the-shoulder fashion that reminded some of his old nemesis, the late Democratic speaker, Tip O'Neill. "In the end," said his longtime comrade, Bob Walker, "what direction Newt decides to take us is the direction we are most likely to go." To the surprise of some who had viewed Gingrich as a hard-liner during his days in the minority, his voice in internal disputes was more often than not one of moderation.

BACK in early February, Gingrich had visited the Appropriations Committee for a closed-door meeting with Chairman Bob Livingston of Louisiana and his thirteen subcommittee chairmen, known collectively as "the cardinals." It was not by chance or seniority that Big Bob Livingston sat in the chairman's seat. The six-foot-six former prosecutor had been handpicked for the assignment by Gingrich and Armey, who passed over three committee members with more seniority in their search for someone they considered tough enough for the job. Ralph Regula of Ohio seemed a shade too soft and moderate. C. W. Bill Young of Florida had other missions more important to him. And John Myers of Indiana had failed the Gingrich test set up before the 1994 elections: He did not raise enough money or help the Republican team with sufficient time and energy.

Livingston not only met the financial challenge, raising nearly $150,000 for the party in 1994, he also had a personal connection to both top leaders: he was a fishing buddy of Armey's and shared an alma mater—Tulane—with Gingrich. While not a member of the Just Us Chickens gang that had plotted the revolution, his conservative credentials were solid, though some activists on the right complained when he retained a few committee staffers from the Democratic regime.

Livingston's ideology and strength would be tested soon enough, which was the purpose of Gingrich's visit. The speaker reminded the chairman and his cardinals that they would be making deep cuts in programs they had funded for years. "You're going to be in the forefront of the revolution," he said. "You have the toughest jobs in the House. If you don't want to do it, tell me." He said that he would meet individually with each cardinal to discuss the leadership agenda for each of the thirteen bills they would be shepherding through committee and onto the House floor. There would be no confusion about the philosophy of every bill and Gingrich's priorities. He instructed the cardinals to write him letters reaffirming their commitment. "It was Newt's way of letting us know we were in for a tough load," said Livingston, who sent his letter back with the satiric signoff, "Love and kisses!"

To make their task more difficult, Livingston and his cardinals were being asked to accommodate a sweeping legislative agenda that normally would be handled by the committees responsible for authorizing programs. The leadership had decided that the money bills had to be used for that purpose because the normal flow of legislation was impossible: Too much time had been consumed on the Contract with America. Under what were called the "Armey Protocols," established by the majority leader as a legislative strategy, authorizing committee chairmen were instructed to work with the appropriations cardinals to agree on policy legislation that would be pushed through the money bills. "You'll get a lot of stuff done, but using the appropriations process," Armey had told the committee chairmen. Aside from the press of time, there were also political reasons for the strategy. Stand-alone bills on such issues as abortion, workplace safety, and environmental regulation would be easier for President Clinton to veto than appropriations measures needed to keep the government running.

There had always been a certain amount of legislative language slipped into money bills, but nothing of this magnitude and scope. From his perspective as former chairman and ranking Democrat, David Obey viewed it as a raw power play by the Gingrich team to "stick a lot of things in that they ideologically lust for." The corporate interests who support the revolution, Obey said, "see this as a quick way to get through the legislative process without letting people know what the hell they are doing." Indeed, many of the proposals by Cass Ballenger to dismantle the workplace health and safety bureaucracy and by Minority Whip Tom DeLay to weaken federal environmental regulations found their way into the appropriations bills.

While Livingston agreed with the ideology driving all of this, the loading of his bills nonetheless became an increasing source of irritation for him. An expressive man, whose good humor is occasionally interrupted by volcanic explosions, Livingston reached his limit early one spring morning when Ernest Istook, a conservative Republican from Oklahoma, presented the committee with a thirteen-page amendment whose intent was to "defund the left" by barring government money from going to public interest nonprofit institutions. When a Democrat demanded that the amendment be read in full, a process that consumed nearly an hour during an all-night committee session, Livingston stormed from his seat and placed a telephone call to Speaker Gingrich, who had been asleep in a hotel room in California.

"God damn it! This is going to sink our bill," Livingston screamed into the telephone. "Get it off. Fix it! You guys are piling a lot of crap on my bill!" Gingrich offered Livingston a sympathetic ear, but that was all. The leadership wanted the Istook provisions. The process would continue. Livingston calmed down and supported the amendment.

FOR much of the summer, Gingrich played the role of appropriations overseer, intervening when a dispute arose that only he could resolve. At times he seemed torn between the ideals of the revolution, his own pet political interests, and the practicality of moving legislation. Kasich and the New Federalists, led by freshman Sam Brownback of Kansas, challenged the leadership on several issues: funding for the Commerce Department and the National Endowment for the Arts, both of which they wanted abolished; and on a "lockbox" provision that would ensure that savings from appropriations cuts would only be used to reduce the deficit. Gingrich at times chastised Kasich for being overly aggressive, but he also helped negotiate deals placating the freshmen on their issues.

When the appropriations bill for housing, veterans, and independent agencies began moving through the committee in July, the speaker emerged as more of a dealmaker. At stake was a bill that always requires legislative agility because of the disparate interests it funds, a task made even more sensitive because of the cuts needed to reach the balanced budget goals. Every dollar given to one agency meant one less for the others, and in this case many of the agencies represented traditional Republican constituencies such as aerospace contractors and veterans. But there were risks to gutting programs in housing and the environment that were important to the smaller bloc of urban moderates needed to fill out any GOP majority. They were also important, though Gingrich may not have calculated it then, to his adversary in the White House whom he ultimately would have to face if any of his agenda was to become law.

In charge of this balancing act was "cardinal" Jerry Lewis, a silver-haired moderate from Southern California who had been ousted from a party leadership post by conservatives a few years ago. Lewis was one of the reasons Gingrich had demanded loyalty letters from the cardinals, but he quickly proved his willingness to adapt to the tough new order. His subcommittee planned to make such deep cuts that virtually all of the diverse interests, including veterans and NASA space center supporters, threatened to scuttle a bill central to the Republican pledge to shrink government.

Gingrich, a technocrat who decorated his office with dinosaur bones and teeth, had a special interest in space and science programs and wanted to find more money for those programs without upsetting the other groups. First he used a bookkeeping maneuver to fatten the health care allotment for veterans. Assured that the veterans' lobby would then not complain about more money going to space and science, Gingrich persuaded Lewis to restore funding for space centers in Virginia, Alabama, and Maryland, the homes of legislators whose votes were needed to pass the bill. The speaker showed a moderate impulse in his final compromise. The Department of Housing and Urban Development (HUD) had long been a target of many conservatives. Lewis, noting recent examples of HUD corruption and waste, unhesitantly pushed his panel to cut its budget by one-quarter.

But the party's moderates decided to take their stand. Leading the way was Rick Lazio of New York, who marched twenty-five of his Lunch Bunch allies into DeLay's whip office to protest cuts they described as punitive to society's most helpless. Before long, Lazio was invited to a meeting with Gingrich and Lewis, at which he appealed for more money to subsidize housing for the disabled, the elderly, and people with AIDS. As Lewis argued against the move, he seemed to reverse roles with his old conservative adversary Gingrich. The last thing Republicans needed, the speaker said, was to be portrayed as turning their backs on "the poorest of the poor," as they had in the school lunch debacle. Gingrich added the word "compassion" to his lexicon, urged a course of moderation, and restored $600 million for special needs housing before the bill reached the House floor.

Gingrich assumed that the housing compromise had resolved the problems in Lewis's bill. But one more battle loomed, an environmental fight that surprised the leadership and for a few days stood out as its most glaring defeat. Until then, DeLay and his probusiness allies had carved up twenty-five years of environmental law with the approval of large majorities in the House. The ease and scope of their effort was breathtaking. It took just a few months to halt pending regulations and erect barriers against new ones, weaken clean-water laws, and throw open national forests and the Arctic Refuge to commercial interests. Lewis's bill, which cut EPA spending by a third, and restrained its enforcement powers, encountered little opposition as it moved to the floor for the July vote.

No one paid much attention when Republican Sherwood Boehlert of New York announced that he planned to join Democrats in fighting seventeen provisions tacked onto the bill. Industry was lobbying heavily for these riders, as they are known in legislative jargon. They restricted EPA's use of funds to regulate pesticides in processed foods, curb hazardous emissions from oil refineries and cement kilns, require emergency plans for oil and gas companies, and set limits on arsenic and radon in drinking water. The proposed restrictions achieved through a single spending bill what could take years to pass in the authorizing committees. As the vote neared, Lewis presented such an optimistic forecast of the vote on the EPA riders at a leadership meeting that DeLay and his whips saw no need to poll their members on the issue.

But a few days later, Lewis realized that he had vastly under-estimated support for environmental regulations, and sent word to Gingrich. The speaker left the impression that he was too busy to negotiate the problem himself and suggested that Boehlert and antiregulation westerners meet to work out their differences. With the speaker giving no strong signals, Livingston kept pushing a vote, which ended up defeating the anti-environmental riders, as Boehlert had hoped. Fifty-one Republicans defected on the floor that Friday—one of the largest groups opposing a leadership initia-tive all year. Four of Livingston's cardinals broke ranks and joined the opposition.

Boehlert's rebellion not only startled the House leadership, it also emboldened the White House, which began to realize that it could gain public favor by emphasizing its differences with the revolution on environmental issues. Many Republicans were growing concerned. They were coming back from weekend vis-its with constituents who were saying that the House actions had frightened and alarmed them: They did not want arsenic in their drinking water or toxins in the air.

Whether the outcome would have changed had Gingrich inter-vened is open to question. His inaction was not without its own degree of calculation. The speaker had ambivalent feelings about the EPA provisions. He was somewhat "greener" than his leader-ship allies, especially Armey and DeLay, and concerned that Re-publicans not be viewed as utterly hostile to the environment—a perception that was beginning to become apparent in polls. When Lewis asked for a second vote after a weekend of regrouping, Gingrich said privately that he preferred not to challenge the mod-erates after one of their few victories. But he was out of town the following Monday, and deferred to Armey and DeLay, who wanted a second chance on behalf of business interests and west-ern conservatives eager for the riders. They got lucky the second time around. After DeLay had finished his whip count, he walked up to an Appropriations Committee aide and said, "I'll tell you what I learned today: what this is all about is who's in town." DeLay's side won the revote without changing a single Republican; the difference was absent Democrats.

SINCE the Republicans took control in January, the social conservatives of the party had been pushing for action on the seminal issue of their cause: abortion. The leadership kept putting them off, fearful that abortion would undo the tenuous majority the leadership had relied on to pass the Contract with America by upsetting moderates. Now, in early August, as the massive Labor–HHS bill started rolling through the House, the leadership felt obligated finally to give anti-abortion legislators their chance. "It was payback time," said Livingston.

The leadership's concern that abortion could tear apart the Republican rank-and-file seemed confirmed as the social services vote neared. When Gingrich, Armey, and DeLay met at two o'clock on the afternoon of Tuesday, August 1, the day before the bill was to reach the floor, they saw trouble from both sides. Conservatives had prevailed in committee by adding three abortion-limiting measures to the bill. Moderates were now pushing to add two abortion rights provisions of their own on the floor. One, by Jim Greenwood of Pennsylvania, would restore family planning funds, which had been eliminated in committee by those who said some of that money was used by groups such as Planned Parenthood to sponsor abortions. Another, by Jim Kolbe of Arizona, would provide federal Medicaid funding for abortions in cases of rape and incest in states that limited their own funding to instances where the life of the woman was endangered.

Both sides had signaled the leadership that they would vote against the entire bill unless they were satisfied by the House ruling on which of the amendments they had sponsored would be protected from parliamentary challenges on the House floor. Without a rule specifically waiving them from challenges, all the abortion provisions could be stricken on the House floor because appropriations bills were not supposed to contain language that legislated policy. A leader of the Pro-Life Caucus, Chris Smith of New Jersey, carried a letter signed by more than sixty colleagues committed to killing the rule if its wording went against them.

At four that afternoon in Room H-137 of the Capitol, Gingrich brought together forty members from the two sides and said he would not be forced to choose "between different parts of the family." Either they worked out a compromise, he said, "or we're going to bring this up without a rule"—which would protect none of the amendments from challenge. As Gingrich spoke, aides distributed a list of unauthorized programs that would thus become vulnerable. It was apparent to anti-abortion legislators that they had a lot to lose, and they were upset that Gingrich seemed to be placating the moderates.

"Newt, you're siding with the other side!" fumed Chris Smith.

Gingrich, unfazed, responded: "That's the deal."

Seeing that he could not resolve the dispute immediately, Gingrich recruited Budget Chairman Kasich to mediate a smaller gathering. Four members from each group gathered in Armey's office, and after a few hours of bargaining, a deal was struck. The moderates would get to introduce Greenwood's amendment to restore funds for the family planning programs, but they would give up on the Kolbe amendment on Medicaid payments. The Pro-Life Caucus would have protections for three anti-abortion waivers. "To see Jim Greenwood and Chris Smith shake hands—this was a miracle almost comparable to Fatima," Kasich said.

On Wednesday, August 2, the leadership's rule passed on the House floor, as did Greenwood's amendment, which won the support of fifty-three Republicans, including the appropriations subcommittee chairman overseeing the Labor–HHS bill, moderate John Edward Porter of Illinois. Porter, who had signed the loyalty oath of cardinals to Gingrich at the beginning of the year, found himself walking a fine line between his pledge to the leadership and his moderate instincts. His great fear was that his party would "go so far to one side" on abortion and the environment that "we will lose the mainstream." He defended the bill from outside attacks while trying to moderate it here and there, a task that his colleagues on the other side of the aisle felt was beneath his dignity. Democrat David Obey viewed Porter as "a tragic figure" in the revolution, "a good guy surrounded by extremists."

But the Kasich-brokered compromise on abortion was only temporary. The trouble was not over. DeLay's staff, after polling members all day, discovered the entire bill was endangered and called in a warning to Gingrich's chief of staff, Dan Meyer. "Clear Newt's schedule," DeLay said. "He's going to have to spend a lot of time on this."

At a leadership meeting at eight-fifteen the next morning, DeLay divided the dissatisfied into three groups: anti-abortion lawmakers who hated the Greenwood provision; abortion rights supporters who disliked the bill's other anti-abortion language; and pro-labor members from the Northeast upset with the bill's rollback of labor laws. The whip asked Gingrich to meet with each of the groups, which he did in succession that afternoon from two to four o'clock. Gingrich told the conservatives that they were getting most of what they wanted and no one could ever get 100 percent. With the moderates, he appealed to their sense of unity. It was John Porter's bill, he said. Porter was one of them. He had worked long and hard for it. "Try to be supportive." He acknowledged that there was not much he could do for the members in pro-labor districts. Maybe they could get more legislative protection in the fall.

At 8:30 P.M., a whip count showed forty undecided Republicans still out there, waiting to see how votes went on key amendments before they would say yes or no to the full bill. Among the moderates, fourteen were still listed in the "leaning no" or "hard no" column.

At nine o'clock, twenty-three anti-abortion members of the conservative Family Caucus gathered in a large circle in the Tip O'Neill Room, where their Bible study class usually meets, to go over their concerns one last time. For the first forty-five minutes, they talked about how important the abortion issue was in their campaigns and how they had vowed that they would not compromise once they reached Congress. Could they in good conscience support a measure that allowed for family planning funds that might be used for abortions?

"One of the things we have to be careful about," said Mark Souder of Indiana, "is that power doesn't tempt us to vote for things we don't believe in."

Donald Manzullo of Illinois recalled how Ben Franklin, on another hot summer night at the Constitutional Convention in Philadelphia, called for divine intervention during a deadlock.

"Why doesn't someone start with a prayer and I'll close," said Oklahoma's Tom Coburn. They took turns praying, leaning forward in their chairs with heads bowed and eyes closed, occasionally holding hands. Jay Dickey of Arkansas quoted a verse of scripture from memory. John Ensign of Nevada picked up a Bible and thumbed through it for another appropriate verse.

They returned to the House floor after eleven, reluctantly concluding that a limited victory would be better than none at all. They would all vote for the bill.

"Thank you, God!" Appropriations Chairman Livingston would say later, laughing.

At midnight, the leadership was still searching for the winning margin. Gingrich called a dozen moderates up to his office for a final appeal. His pitch again was for the good of the party, made in the presence of Republican National Committee Chairman Haley Barbour. This was the last big vote before the August break, Gingrich said. "We can go home being one of the most successful first seven months of any congressional majority in history, or we can go home and the story will be that it's starting to come apart, the Republicans are shooting each other, it's starting to unravel. Some of you have been here a very long time and have very safe districts. This is a tough vote for some of our freshmen. If you're going to vote no, some of those people are willing to vote yes. For the good of the team, it would be helpful if we got some of you guys."

Much of Gingrich's attention was focused on Marge Roukema of New Jersey, who entered the room as a "hard no" vote in the whip count. "Don't always expect us to bail you out after you've painted yourselves into an ideological corner," Roukema told the speaker. But she came around, reluctantly, as did the others.

The next day, after his all-night talkathon with Armey and the boys, Gingrich stood before a gathering of the entire Republican membership, which he had convened in Room HC-5 for a celebratory lunch of pizza and soft drinks. Armey and DeLay and John Boehner had already spoken, and now the chant went up, shaking the room: "Newt! Newt! Newt!" There had been much disagreement, Gingrich said, but in the end the House Republicans had shown that the team matters more than the individual. He reflected on how members had compromised in the interests of "looking out for the family." Tears welled in his eyes and there was an eerie quiet in the room as he fought to regain his composure.

WHEN Bob Livingston got home that night, his daughter said that someone from the White House had called. He was exhausted. They were the last people he wanted to talk to right now. But he placed the return call out of curiosity, and was told by a Clinton aide that the president wanted to play golf with Livingston the next day. I'll have to think about that, Livingston said. A minute later he phoned back and accepted.

So there he was, still bone-tired on a Saturday morning, hacking his way from tee to green, the President of the United States serving as his chauffeur, partner, and golf teacher. Livingston had heard about Clinton's charm, but he had never seen it firsthand like this before. The president never stopped shooting the bull. He boasted about how he once outdrove Jack Nicklaus. And he was booming the ball today, too, driving it almost 250 yards straight down the fairway on many holes. "This guy is pretty good," Livingston thought to himself.

For his part, Livingston's game was falling apart. It seemed that the worse he hacked and sliced, the nicer Clinton became. Every now and then, between shots, the president talked shop. The buzz around Washington was about a potential train wreck in the fall. All those appropriations bills coming over to the White House, one less acceptable to the president than the next. No way he could sign that Labor–HHS bill that the Republicans just passed. Maybe they could work things out, do some compromising, meet the policy concerns of Clinton and avoid the train wreck.

Thwack! Sure don't want to have to veto all those bills, said the president. *Hack!* Sure hope you don't, said Livingston, trying to keep his head down. Big Bob ended up in the rough a lot, but he went home with three presidential golf balls.

EIGHT

Hawk versus Hawk

IN THE VOCABULARY of the most expensive aircraft in aviation history, Newt Gingrich seemed stealthy and low observable on the day that his revolution got around to the B-2 bomber. The Army brat who grew up to be a congressional general had convened a meeting of his Republican leadership team at three on the afternoon of June 13 to plot strategy for legislation funding the Pentagon and its industrial contractors. They gathered in Room H-227 of the Capitol, a gilded chamber that had once housed a committee on naval affairs, evoking a military atmosphere befitting this discussion of the nation's defense. Black felt cloth was draped over the table and warlike Viking ships looked down from murals on the groin-vaulted ceiling.

The question at hand was whether the leadership should whip the most controversial weapons system in the defense bill, the B-2 Stealth bomber. "To whip," as a verb in congressional nomenclature, means the leadership takes sides on an issue, counts votes, and exerts varying degrees of pressure to round up a majority. Although the B-2 was, this year at least, a relatively small part of the defense package, its symbolic importance in terms of defining the direction of the conservative revolution transcended the money involved. It represented a significant test of strength between two species of Republican hawks, each of which claimed to be ideological heirs of Ronald Reagan. On one side were the new-breed deficit hawks, also known as "cheap" hawks, and on the other were the traditional defense hawks.

Both were represented at the speaker's leadership table.

The Texans who served as Gingrich's top two lieutenants, Majority Leader Dick Armey and Majority Whip Tom DeLay, were B-2 adherents. The Lone Star delegation had a long history of support for major weapons systems, a commitment in this case bolstered by the presence in Texas of LTV, a major subcontractor that made the B-2's titanium frame. Republican Conference Chairman John Boehner of Ohio was another Stealth man: his district neighbored the Wright-Patterson Air Force Base, headquarters for the B-2 program office. Christopher Cox, the policy committee chair, pushed the cause as a representative from California, where the planes were assembled by Northrop Grumman, the main contractor.

Leading the deficit hawks was John Kasich, the rambunctious chairman of the House Budget Committee, who considered the B-2 a prodigious waste of money with its uncertain strategic mission and sticker price that once reached $2 billion per plane. Kasich, the lead figure in the movement to balance the federal books by the year 2002, was marshaling a growing legion of budget-cutting partisans, especially in the big and brash freshman class, who followed his credo that the Pentagon was not sacrosanct. He had spent six years trying to kill the Stealth bomber, and had nearly done so several times, only to have the radar-evasive aircraft somehow reappear. "What's the difference between the B-2 and Dracula?" he would joke. "Even if you put a stake through the heart of the B-2, it won't die."

Gingrich had sympathy for both sides. Although he had previously signed petitions for the B-2 and would endorse it again this time, he realized that his rank-and-file was more divided on the issue than any other. Many "cheap" hawks, including Kasich, believed that Gingrich in his heart of hearts was closer to them and would not mind if they won. Known for the certitude of his pronouncements, the speaker was now uncharacteristically quiet. His reluctance or inability to shape the B-2 debate stood in marked contrast to the way he normally framed issues and united his membership around his vision. In other areas, his cockiness made colleagues bold; now his ambivalence seemed to reflect the larger uncertainty of House Republicans on how to resolve the competing impulses of national security and fiscal restraint.

Did they have to whip the B-2? Gingrich hesitantly asked his leadership team. "I support the B-2," he said, according to a calendar diary kept by one person in the room. "But I'm a little uncomfortable making it a leadership vote."

Armey presented the case for whipping. Here was a plane, he said, that had been an essential part of the defense buildup that reinvigorated the Pentagon during the 1980s, restored American military supremacy, and accelerated the demise of the Soviet Empire. The huge boomerang-shaped bomber with its 172-foot wingspan was a proud symbol of the Reagan era, a legacy that House Republicans, in their Contract with America, had vowed not to forget. The whipping question was put to a show of hands, which the defense hawks won handily. Gingrich did not vote.

With the leadership officially behind it but with Gingrich playing only a minimal role, legislation keeping the B-2 alive passed the House later that evening, though barely, and despite word from Pentagon officials that their strategic defense plans did not require more Stealth bombers. Another measure appropriating money for the B-2 survived by a margin of only three votes in a second test in September. Those victories made it possible for the House to negotiate to keep the B-2 alive in conference with the Senate, which previously served the role of Stealth resuscitator but this time failed to support the plane.

Kasich had thought that he had the votes to kill the B-2 for good in 1995, and indeed mustered eighty GOP colleagues to his side. It was an abnormally large Republican showing against a major weapons system, and one that might portend a rearrangement of the traditional relationship between Republicans and the Pentagon. "Eighty-one Repubs!" Kasich exclaimed later. "We have a cultural change taking place in this party right now, and this cultural change is important not to lose sight of. You do realize that this is about corporate welfare as well. We have a force inside the party now that understands that corporate welfare needs to be cut and that defense industries are part of corporate welfare. That just because the Pentagon wants something doesn't mean they ought to get it."

But the story of how the B-2 survived was illuminating in its own right, revealing that the military-industrial complex can still be an imposing force in the political world and has a vast array of tools it can use to win support from both parties.

The lobbying campaign conducted by Northrop Grumman and its congressional sponsors tapped a vast network of hundreds of subcontractors and thousands of vendors spread through forty-eight states, a million-dollar advertising campaign that drew on polls and focus groups, campaign contributions from Northrop Grumman totaling $385,000 in 1995 (70 percent of it to Republican congressmen), an office-to-office touring delegation of retired generals, and letters of support from seven former secretaries of defense. "You have the Seven Secretaries—like the Seven Wonders of the World," Kasich said sarcastically. "They used that against us all the time. Melvin Laird's position on the B-2, written while having a bowl of soup out at Burning Tree Country Club." In addition, the general disarray of congressional Democrats, the specific economic concerns of California, and the sensitive presidential politics of that crucial state all assisted the B-2 cause.

IN the conference room of Northrop Grumman's office in suburban Washington, chief lobbyist Bob Helm opened his regular Monday morning meeting on November 14, 1994, on an unusually optimistic note. A few days earlier, Republicans had captured the House in the midterm elections, assuring major changes in the scorecard of congressional players dealing with the B-2.

Reduced to minority party status was Armed Services Committee Chairman Ronald Dellums, the Berkeley liberal who had fought for years to kill the bomber in an odd couple partnership with conservative Kasich. Dellums and Kasich had successfully curtailed the production line of B-2s from an original squadron of 132 down to 75, and finally apparently freezing the number at 20. The new chairman of the renamed National Security Committee would be Floyd Spence of South Carolina, a quintessential southern defense hawk whose office was a veritable museum of military might, with portraits of generals lining the walls and his cabinets stocked with miniature armaments. Working alongside Spence as chairman of the weapons procurement subcommittee would be an even older friend of the B-2: San Diego conservative Duncan Hunter, who spent two years as an Army Ranger in Vietnam, and now represented some of the small businesses benefiting from production of a major weapons system in Southern California.

Helm made note of the shifting political winds in the House, a body all but written off by Northrop in recent years because of Dellums's control of military procurement. "We're going to be dealing with a leadership that is friendly towards the B-2," he told the group of fifteen lobbyists and outside consultants assigned to the plane in Washington. For years it had been the Senate, with hawkish Democrats Sam Nunn of Georgia and Daniel K. Inouye of Hawaii running defense panels, where the contractor went to keep the bomber alive. Now the House Republicans, with a strong defense plank in their Contract with America, seemed to be Northrop Grumman's most likely friends in need.

Soon enough, Helm's hopes were confirmed. Shortly after the Republicans took control in January 1995, he visited Hunter. "I think we need more B-2s," the congressman said. Helm could not agree more. The twentieth and possibly final B-2 would soon be coming off a production line that had slowed so much in recent years that half the supplier base had been rendered inactive. Congress barely kept it alive in 1994, providing $125 million while the Pentagon undertook a study of long-term bomber needs. This was the critical year. Unless Congress rejuvenated the B-2 process, the company believed, restarting the production network would become prohibitively expensive. Northrop Grumman was so eager to keep producing the B-2, which had accounted for about $40 billion to the firm and its subcontractors over the years, that it now offered to sell the Air Force twenty more bombers for $15.3 billion.

In the big-figure world of high-tech defense contracts, that was a discount price. Helm passed it along to Hunter.

The offer had natural supporters in Hunter and two fellow Southern Californians, Congressmen Jerry Lewis and Buck McKeon, who in late January organized a B-2 Task Force with pro-defense Democrats Norm Dicks and Ike Skelton. The lawmakers were linked by their service on key defense committees and by vital interests in the B-2. The plane is assembled in McKeon's district in suburban Los Angeles. Many Northrop Grumman workers live in Lewis's adjacent district. The bomber flies on wings made by Boeing in Dicks's state of Washington, and seven of them are parked at Whiteman Air Force Base in Skelton's Missouri.

The quartet served as the driving force behind legislation providing $493 million to the B-2 in 1995, enough to provide components for two more planes beyond the twenty but serving in essence as a down payment for twenty more. Gathering regularly in Lewis's office, the B-2 proponents discussed how to overcome the post–cold war defense lull and the penurious ethic of Republican freshmen. By February, Northrop's Bob Helm was invited to every fourth meeting and asked to report on the grass-roots efforts of B-2 suppliers, the wide network of large defense firms and tiny machine shops that Lewis identified early on as a vital connection to legislators who needed a reason to vote for the bomber. "Let their members know there are actual jobs related to this," Lewis importuned Helm.

Lists were compiled of every vendor connected to the B-2 in every congressional district. The list of vendors in Buck McKeon's district demonstrated how it could be said that the B-2 production ran the alphabet of the American economy: Antelope Vacuum, Bob's Upholstery Shop, Clark Pest Control, Dale's Hitchin' Station, Elite Car Wash, Frank's Radio Service, Great American Business Systems, High Desert Graphics, Imperial Tool Company, Johnson Auto Center, Kwik Key Service, Lockheed Corporation, Marshall Tool and Supply, New Hampshire Ball Bearings, Optronics Specialty Company, Pickus Repair Service, Rockwell International, Space Age Control, Thermax Wire, Valley Iron Steel

Fabricator, Wesco Aircraft, Xenotronix Incorporated—all part of the B-2 vendor network, with subcontracts totaling $149 million in one congressional district alone.

Before the House leadership began whipping, the B-2 task force and Northrop Grumman started doing it on their own. Lobbyists and congressional vote counters were provided with "whip cards" for each member, listing the number of district businesses involved in B-2 work and their sales. Black lawmakers were informed if suppliers were minority-owned and female lawmakers if they were owned by women. Congressmen were given batlike Stealth models and coffee mugs. The whip cards were reprinted in different colors to track the status of lawmakers and determine if they needed bolstering by a visit from a local business group or a famous retired general such as Charles Horner, overseer of the air war in Desert Storm. Northrop Grumman launched campaign funds like heat-seeking missiles. The chief adherents of the B-2, Democrat and Republican, were rewarded with donations of at least $5,000. About $50,000 was targeted in more partisan fashion at the group of lawmakers whom Kasich most hoped to win over to his side: GOP freshmen. Democratic first-termers, by contrast, received a mere $2,000 in total contributions.

ONE summer day in his congressional office, John Kasich leaped from his chair and bounded over to a cabinet where he kept his own model version of the B-2 Stealth bomber. It was a wooden stand with nothing attached, at least no visible plane.

"Do you see the B-2?" Kasich asked. "*Do you see it?* See—it's working!"

It was an old joke first coined by a military mathematician named William J. Perry, the same man who later served as President Clinton's secretary of defense and who in a previous incarnation, during the Carter administration in the late 1970s, was an undersecretary at the Pentagon who became known as "the Godfather of Stealth." In Stealth technology for fighters, attack planes, and bombers, aircraft were constructed using materials and designs to minimize their radar signatures: the massive B-2 would theoretically show up as nothing larger than a hawk. It required technological perfection, the creation of nine hundred new processes and materials, and melding of forty thousand parts in such a way that if they were off by a hair it ruined the effect. This was all a big secret from Perry's days through the late years of the Reagan presidency, when the first plane rolled off the production line. From the Pentagon's fifth-floor D-Ring, where a study was conducted of low observables, to Northrop's Palmdale and Pico Rivera plants in California where the planes were assembled, everything was done in what was known as "the black world" of SAR, secret access required. Most members of Congress had no idea how much the planes cost.

Kasich first learned of the estimated cost of building 132 B-2s at a meeting of the Armed Services Committee in 1988. He was stunned by the $72 billion price tag, and soon formed an alliance to kill it with Ronald Dellums, the Bay Area liberal he had befriended lifting weights in the House gym. One night when they were dinner guests at the home of liberal Democrat Tom Downey of New York, Kasich turned to Dellums and said, "You know, Ron, I really don't like this B-2 bomber. It just doesn't make any sense to me. I can't figure out any way that we can get rid of it, but maybe we ought to cut it back."

"Why can't we get rid of it?" Dellums asked, surprised and encouraged by Kasich's position. Why not? thought Kasich, and the effort began. The partnership did not sit well with old-line Republican defense hawks. "It was my being a sellout by cooperating with Ron Dellums and people like *that*," Kasich recalled. "They said I talk all the right talk and say all the right things, but here I am cooperating with the enemy to destroy the defense of the United States."

The original policy argument for the B-2 was that it could bring the lethal power of a much larger force with fewer pilots exposed to danger, and that its technology would foil the Soviets or force them to waste money to counteract it. The B-2 was conceived with a specific mission in mind: To deliver nuclear weapons against the

Soviet Union. That mission, like almost everything else about the plane, was refashioned as the world changed dramatically over the long period it was being designed and produced.

After wounding the B-2 for six years, citing a history of cost overruns, late deliveries, unacceptable performance tests, and radar glitches that made the plane incapable of functioning safely during rainstorms, Kasich thought that now he had the support finally to kill it. The Clinton administration did not want the plane. The Pentagon, now run by William Perry, said it did not need the plane. A long-term bomber study conducted by Perry's old assistant, Paul Kaminski, another early Stealth devotee, concluded that the twenty current B-2s were "sufficient for anticipated scenarios," and that defense money would be more wisely spent on accurate guided missiles or upgrades of older bombers. But B-2 devotees who had spent decades turning to the Pentagon for support now dismissed it as a political tool of the Democratic White House. When Kasich showed the report to Duncan Hunter, he replied, "Well, what do you expect the Pentagon to say? Of course they don't want the plane." Kasich interpreted the response to mean: Who can trust the generals? It was the first time he had heard that argument from a hawk.

There were other variables that made Kasich's task more difficult than he first expected and that ultimately led to his narrow defeat. Liberal Democrats who normally opposed spending on major weapons systems were so upset with Republican cuts in social programs and desperate to save jobs in their districts that they became susceptible to Northrop Grumman's job entreaties. David Obey, a longtime B-2 opponent, said he understood why some of his colleagues, including many members of the Congressional Black Caucus, ended up supporting the plane. "This crap is continuing to be built because this country is not doing what it was doing at the end of World War II, when we had millions of GIs coming back and a potentially huge economic problem. We didn't have any place to put them, so we parked them in colleges and trade schools and upgraded their skills. Today we are not doing any of that stuff. So members from districts with defense plants are forced to try to squeeze dollars out for these unneeded projects because there is no national strategy to move to other things besides the Pentagon."

Where was Clinton's White House now? The administration, though officially opposed to more B-2 spending, "went quiet" during a crucial period before the appropriations vote, a withdrawal that many on both sides attributed to the realization that California was crucial to Clinton's reelection chances.

Kasich also had trouble with the large Republican freshman class. They were gung-ho with Kasich on budget cutting, but unable to unite on questions of defense.

For symbolic as well as vote-counting purposes it was important to Northrop Grumman to forge a Republican united front from California, home of the B-2. Frank Riggs, a freshman reformer from the northern coast, received the full treatment, but proved to be the biggest challenge. During the 1994 campaign, Duncan Hunter helped Riggs raise money over the phone, getting Northrop officials on the line and handing them over to the candidate after introductions. "It was, hello, how are you. Get acquainted," Riggs recalled. "They were working on this back then, looking ahead, trying to get a sense of the lay of the land."

Offers for help intensified after his election and as the B-2 votes approached. "That part wasn't too subtle," according to Riggs. "It happens at the Capitol Hill Club. They hear we're having an event and they offer to be there, offer to help out, offer to not only come and contribute but get others to come and contribute, to sell other tickets." He was also constantly visited by members of his delegation. The pressure, he said, was "to look at the B-2 in the context of a parochial program for California, a jobs program. . . . They do stress what they view as the merits of the program, but when you cut to the chase, it is, 'Hey, look, this is a real important program to me, my district, my constituents, and our state.' "

Riggs accepted Northrop's campaign contributions and listened to his congressional elders from California, whom he respected greatly. But he was not swayed. He was one of thirty Republican freshmen, out of the seventy-one voting, who spurned the B-2. The vote, he said, was "a pretty good test, perhaps even the acid test, as to whether or not we're going to be cheap hawks and whether or not we're going to strive for this concept of shared sacrifice." The support Kasich received from the newcomers was not as large as he had hoped for, but it marked a significant generational trend nonetheless. The freshmen arrived after the cold war and with less military experience than their elders. The number of veterans in Congress was decreasing steadily. Before 1992, half of all House members were veterans. Of the freshmen that year, 90 of 110 had no military experience. In 1994, 65 of 87 freshmen had not served.

Freshman Steve Chabot of Ohio voted against the B-2 even though the Northrop Grumman lists showed that his district ranked sixth in the nation in subcontracting funds from the project—more than $305 million. John Boehner talked to him, General Horner visited him, but he decided the plane was too expensive. Steve Largent of Oklahoma voted against the B-2 despite a vow that he had made to himself that he would "move to the right" when he reached Washington and support a strong national defense. Then, he said, he compared U.S. defense spending with the budgets of other countries and was struck by what he called "the tremendous imbalance." He called the vote against the B-2 a way to send the military a message from the new Congress: "This is not just a rubber stamp: 'How much do you want? How much do you need? Here's a check.' We're not going to be that way."

ONE day Kasich intends to escort his mentor Gingrich across the Potomac for a four-hour session with Pentagon brass. For the first time in his career, Kasich believed that some reformers there actually liked and respected him. Changing the congressional culture on the military will take time, he said, but it will happen, and he expects Gingrich to be a key player when it does. He has heard the speaker claim that he is a cheap hawk. "Newt is a Pentagon reformer," said Kasich, known for his rock-and-roll approach to life. "He always lectures me: 'Don't you think I'm going to take a backseat to you!' I say, 'Newt, did you ever hear that album by Keith Richards? Of course you didn't, Newt, but the title is *Talk Is Cheap.*"

NINE

The Hammer

IN THE ANNALS of the House Republican Revolution, a pivotal moment came when an unsuspecting corporate lobbyist strolled down the marble corridors of the first floor of the Capitol, made a right turn into the suite of the majority whip, and entered the inner chamber of Tom DeLay, whose aggressive style had earned him the nickname "the Hammer." The Texas congressman was standing at his desk that afternoon, examining a document that listed the amounts and percentages of money that the four hundred largest political action committees had contributed to Republicans and Democrats over the previous two years. Those who gave heavily to the GOP were labeled "Friendly." The others were "Unfriendly." When DeLay caught sight of his visitor, he glanced down at his list again, leafed through it, then looked up and smiled. "See you're in the book," he said. At first the lobbyist was not sure where his group stood, but DeLay helped clear up the confusion. By the time the lobbyist left the whip's office, he knew that to be a friend of the Republican leadership his group would have to give the party a lot more money.

Soon the word spread around town about the Hammer and his book. The word was that you walked into DeLay's office, past the big bullwhip hanging on his wall, and encountered the money book—actually a plastic folder—on the coffee table in front of you. It was purposely left out in the open to impart a clear message: We know who our friends are. The Hammer cares deeply about this book. If he looks in it and discovers that you gave too much to Democrats, you don't get in to see him. Get rated in the "Unfriendly" category, you don't get in. Keep a liberal Democrat on retainer as your Washington agent, you don't get in.

Part of the word was apocryphal. Did lobbyists visiting DeLay's office have to initial their contribution totals like a parent signing a child's report card? Not really. But the whip encouraged that touch of mythology, believing it made his job easier. When an aide once asked whether efforts should be made to quell the legend, DeLay leaned back in his chair, laughed quietly to himself, and said, "No, let it get bigger."

Inside the House Republican leadership, DeLay's job is to be the enforcer on issues of money and politics. His mission is to ensure that money flows along the same stream as policy, that the pro-business deregulatory agenda of the House Republicans receives the undivided financial support of the corporate interests that most benefit from it. His motto is an unabashedly blunt interpretation of the dicta of Speaker Newt Gingrich: "If you want to play in our revolution, you have to live by our rules."

The role of money in the revolution was somewhat obscured during the first year of Republican rule by debates over balanced budgets and the reshaping of the federal government, but it was a part of that larger struggle. Money was at the center of Gingrich's transformation of the House. With the new alignment of ideological allies in the business and political worlds, there were unparalleled opportunities for both the people who give the money and the people who receive it. It was such an obvious quid pro quo that it went almost unnoticed. From House Republicans came measures that gratified industry: weakening environmental standards, loosening workplace safety rules, resuscitating the B-2 bomber, limiting the legal liability of corporations, defunding nonprofit groups that present an opposing view. From the beneficiaries of that legislation come millions of dollars in campaign contributions.

Yet money also became the source of increasing tension among

House Republicans and presented a conflict that threatened to undo the revolution. The contradiction, in essence, was between classic Republican ideology and new-fangled conservative populist reform. Upon taking power, one wing of the party, symbolized by DeLay, wanted to collect as much corporate money as possible to sustain and expand the revolution. Another wing, led by moderates and Republican freshmen and more closely attuned to the reform agenda of Ross Perot, feared that the raw accumulation of money would disillusion voters who brought the Republicans to power to change the traditional ways of doing business in Washington. Speaker Gingrich, the leader of the revolution, found himself caught in the middle of these two forces—aware, people around him said, that the length of his tenure could depend in part on his ability to resolve the conflict.

The Republican takeover of Congress, in any case, set in motion a historic shift in campaign giving. Four decades without power had reduced the House Republican operation to a sputtering financial clunker. As recently as 1993, the National Republican Congressional Committee was millions of dollars in debt and verging on bankruptcy. Now the revolution was running a formidable money machine. By "playing offense" all the time, as DeLay described it, and using a combination of tenacity, collaboration, cheerleading, and intimidation, they began soliciting contributions from the corporate world in unprecedented fashion.

The turnaround has been dramatic. House Republicans raised nearly $60 million in 1995, nearly twice the amount of Democrats. Sixty-one percent of the money from corporate and labor PACs went to the revolution's victors, a vivid contrast to the previous election cycle when two of every three PAC dollars went to the ruling Democrats. The trend is evident in all industries, even those with traditional ties to the Democrats. The Transportation Political Education League, for example, gave only 3 percent to the Republicans in 1994 but 30 percent in 1995. The number-one contributor to the GOP in 1995, United Parcel Service, which worked closely with DeLay and the leadership in fighting federal workplace safety regulations, also made a decisive partisan transformation, going from 47 percent Democratic to 62 percent Republican in one year.

The once threadbare NRCC meanwhile raised a record $34.6 million in 1995, more than three times as much as its Democratic counterpart. Its two elite organizations, which offer private sessions with House leaders at the Capitol Hill Club, were suddenly fat and happy: 250 corporations and political action committees joined the House Council at $5,000 apiece and 150 enrolled in the Congressional Forum for $15,000 to $25,000 each. Bill Paxon, the NRCC's chairman, who described himself as a cheerleader in contrast to DeLay's role as the enforcer, estimated that he has met privately with more than four-fifths of the chief executive officers of Fortune 500 companies to make his pitch. "If you believe in the revolution and what's happening, then it's time to follow common sense," Paxon would tell them. "Why do you support the enemy? Why do you give money to people who are out there consciously every day trying to undermine what's good for you?" He rarely left without a financial pledge.

More than $6 million in NRCC receipts came in unrestricted contributions known as "soft money," used for party rebuilding efforts, voter drives, and policy initiatives. Leading the way in the soft-money realm in 1995 were tobacco companies, which felt threatened by unprecedented environmental and consumer regulation from the Clinton administration. The Food and Drug Administration (FDA) was considering regulating cigarettes as drug-delivery devices. Clinton had delivered a speech calling for a crackdown on tobacco sales to juveniles. Federal workplace regulators were holding hearings on whether smoking should be banned on the job. In response to all that, tobacco interests gave a record $675,000 to the House GOP campaign committee, more than tripling the amount they gave to House Democrats. Philip Morris and RJR Nabisco topped the soft-money list for all Republican election committees, totaling $1.7 million, compared to $325,000 to Democratic operations.

In the midst of this boom, the leaders of the House delved into the money game themselves. Gingrich, DeLay, Armey, and Boehner all established separate PACs with goals of raising millions more apiece. Gingrich's new PAC, dubbed "Monday Morning" in honor of a refrain from his acceptance speech, raised $500,000 from corporate interests in just six months of 1995. Advised by kitchen cabinets of industry lobbyists, these leadership fund-raising operations will distribute funds to Republican congressional candidates, strengthening the bond between the revolution and industry while reinforcing the loyalty of House colleagues to Gingrich and his lieutenants.

The rambunctious freshman class, seventy-three Republican newcomers who considered themselves the vanguard of the revolution, proved as ambitious in the fund-raising realm as elsewhere. They bumped up the average price of a fund-raising ticket to $1,000, fourfold from the previous term, hired professional consultants to run their events and solicit contributions, and formed steering committees of lobbyists to advise them. Most of them liquidated their campaign debts in the first ten months of their first term, and by the start of their second year, fifty of them belonged to the NRCC's Hundred Thousand Dollar Club, having at least that much cash ready for 1996. The Republican freshmen raised an average of nearly $300,000 in the first year, more than doubling their receipts from PACs from the previous nonelection year.

Even reform-minded newcomers who opposed PACs ended up pursuing them aggressively. Sam Brownback of Kansas solicited Washington lobbyists to contribute to a fund-raising event for him soon after he returned from Ross Perot's United We Stand convention in August. There, the farmer's son had given a speech denouncing the Washington lobbying scene as a "domestication process where you bring in new, fresh legislators and then you start to try to tame them and assist them with gifts and meals and trips almost like you would a horse with a sugar cube." Several lobbyists who received Brownback's fund-raising invitation angrily turned him down. But it was only a temporary setback. Nearly 40 percent of the Kansan's $200,000 reelection kitty came from PACs.

Taking all this in with sardonic admiration, one trade association president, a longtime Democrat, said the aggressiveness of the House Republicans left him breathless, surpassing even the fundraising talents of the Democrats in the 1980s under the tutelage of former Democratic Congressional Campaign Committee Chairman Tony Coelho, who also wooed business interests with legislative wish lists. There was another difference between then and now, said this veteran of both Washington fund-raising epochs. "The Republicans have a wonderful situation. They don't have to prostitute themselves. They are ideologically in sync" with the corporate PACs. "Every politician dreams of being able to meet your conscience and raise money at the same time."

IT was only a few days into the revolution in January 1995 when Tom DeLay turned to one of his most trusted allies in the lobbying community, David Rehr of the National Beer Wholesalers Association, and said, "I want you to do something with the freshmen just to get them on the right course." Rehr was considered part of the team, a member of a small group of Washington lobbyists who had remained loyal to the Republicans throughout the long period of Democratic control. In the 1994 election, he helped DeLay coach GOP challengers by making campaign videotapes and raise millions of dollars for them, indebting the winners to vote later for DeLay as majority whip. Rehr's informal duties now included serving as PAC adviser to both DeLay and the NRCC.

In response to DeLay's request, Rehr held a seminar at NRCC headquarters next to the Capitol Hill Club. He entitled it "Seven Steps in Liquidating Your Debt and Building for the Future"—a lecture attended by more than one-quarter of the freshman class. Rehr instructed them to set up steering committees of PAC supporters to be their "eyes and ears" in the Washington community. He suggested that they contact the NRCC and House committee chairmen for a list of PACs relevant to their committee assignments. Make contacts personally, Rehr advised the freshmen.

PACs wanted to hear from them directly. If a PAC opposed them during the campaign, they should not take it personally. Those PACs, he said, should now be considered "additional prospects."

Rehr was among a new breed of Capitol Hill operators on the rise—young, ideological, and fervently committed to the House revolution and its two primary bankers, DeLay and Paxon. The lobbyists span the corporate world, commanding networks of business allies along with large PACs of their own organizations. Dan Mattoon of BellSouth, another lecturer at the NRCC seminar, was the leadership's main link to local telephone companies. Bob Rusbuldt, a top insurance lobbyist, tapped the financial resources of the related fields of mortgage banking and real estate. Jim Boland of Philip Morris drew from the tobacco industry and its food subsidiaries. Free-lance lobbyists such as Bruce Gates, who steered the Project Relief lobbying effort for DeLay's regulatory freeze, brought lists of diverse corporate clients and new fund-raising networks, as did former Republican White House aides Nick Calio and Gary Andres.

The lines of power and money were being redrawn all across Washington. It was a time for "cashing in," as a PAC director close to Speaker Gingrich put it, and also a time for "getting right." Lobbyists whose PACs or clients once gave heavily to Democrats were eager to show they found religion. Late at night at one of the steak and cigar restaurants fashionable along Pennsylvania Avenue, a lobbyist approached one of DeLay's political aides, Bill Jarrell, and pleaded to be restored to good graces. "Man," he said. "Just want to tell you, we've given like seventy percent to you guys now." Corporations with sensitive agendas on Capitol Hill, including Philip Morris, Monsanto, and Ford, elevated Republicans to top jobs in their Washington offices. One drug company hired a Democrat to head its office, but after he was unmasked at a DeLay fund-raiser, he called the whip's office the next day to plead that his firm not be scorned by the House Republicans. His position was only temporary, he said, and he would soon be replaced by someone more aligned with the revolution.

DeLay's shop launched what came to be known as the "K Street Strategy," named for the downtown Washington avenue lined with lobbying headquarters, law firms, and trade associations. The strategy was to pressure those firms to remove Democrats from top jobs and replace them with Republicans. "High-level jobs are being watched as closely as money," said a DeLay aide. Head-hunters began calling DeLay's office in search of recommendations. When one corporation lobbyist sought a meeting with the whip, DeLay telephoned the firm's top executive and complained that his agent in Washington was "a hard-core liberal." If the company wanted to get in to see him, DeLay added, "you need to hire a Republican." The hard-core liberal lobbyist was soon transferred to London. In his next meeting with DeLay, the CEO noted, "We took care of the problem."

Not long after taking power, DeLay received a group of visiting Texas doctors, who brought along a Washington lobbyist for the American Medical Association. Having never met the lobbyist, DeLay quietly asked one of the doctors, "Is he a Republican?" Told he was not, the whip replied, "Then get me one." When the National Association of Homebuilders had the audacity to make a switch in the other direction, replacing chief lobbyist Bob Bannister, who had been a friend of the revolution, with Jerry Howard, whose politics were termed "suspect," the association lost its seat at the table of the Thursday Group, the weekly strategy session with business and trade association leaders hosted by GOP Conference Chairman Boehner.

"There are just a lot of people down on K Street who gained their prominence by being Democrat and supporting the Democrat cause, and they can't regain their prominence unless they get us out of here," DeLay said of the K Street Strategy. "We're just following the old adage of punish your enemies and reward your friends. We don't like to deal with people who are trying to kill the revolution. We know who they are. The word is out."

At times DeLay worked in tandem with fellow Texan Armey to spread the word. DeLay focused on power and money in

Washington, Armey on money and ideology on a broader scale. It infuriated the majority leader that so many Fortune 500 corporations that he thought should have been supporting the revolution were using their philanthropy to arm the opposition. He wrote a letter to dozens of corporate executives blasting them for giving money to liberal public advocacy groups. "One might expect corporate contributions to favor advocacy on behalf of free market principles," Armey wrote. "But the evidence suggests the opposite: big business firmly behind the welfare state." Armey included with his letter a copy of *Patterns of Corporate Philanthropy,* a conservative publication that rated corporations by the ideology of their giving patterns. The study concluded that the liberal left received $3.42 for every $1.00 that went to the right.

Republican leaders sometimes had to choose among friends, and money may have been a factor. When the Commerce Committee voted on a sweeping telecommunications bill in May 1995, for example, its legislation appeared to favor AT&T and other long-distance firms over the regional Bell companies. A last-minute amendment by Chairman Thomas Bliley would have complicated entry of the seven regional Bells into the long-distance market. AT&T has a plant in Bliley's Richmond district and a new PAC profile; reversing a past preference for Democrats, it gave 58 percent to GOP lawmakers in the first seven months of 1995. But the baby Bells, with lobbyist Mattoon leading the pack, came from a strong political position when they appealed the decision. As a group they bested AT&T in PAC contributions to Republicans by more than two to one.

Help came from Paxon and deputy whip Denny Hastert of Illinois, both Commerce Committee members who had voted for the Bliley provision as part of the May bill. They changed their minds after hearing from Bell lobbyists, and argued for a change at a Speaker's Advisory Group meeting in early July, contending that the Bells would be prevented from competing. Gingrich directed Bliley to "rescrub" the bill, and by mid-July the Bliley provision was deleted. On July 19, Nynex contributed

$100,000 in soft money to the NRCC, boosting the contributions of unrestricted funds to Paxon's committee to four times those received by rival Democrats for the year. At about the same time, Pacific Telesis Group's chief executive hosted an intimate fund-raiser for Gingrich at his San Francisco home that raised $20,000.

Paxon explained later that he changed sides because of a "driving passion" for deregulation, not out of fund-raising calculations: "I haven't sat down with a legislative calendar and said, this is the time to go after this industry group." Apparently not taking any chances, AT&T tripled its PAC contributions to House Republicans in the last five months of 1995.

Some fund-raising efforts were less than subtle. Leaders of the revolution and their disciples have often written letters to industry PACs letting them know that they are carefully monitoring their contributions. One letter was sent out October 23, 1995, from the entire Oklahoma GOP delegation, telling the corporate lobbyists that they expected them to support their colleague, freshman Tom Coburn, in his tough reelection race. "As you are courted by others to get involved in this race, we want to make our position clear," the letter read. "We strongly support our good friend and colleague, Tom Coburn, and we will be unified as we work on his behalf. We trust you will join us in our effort and certainly not oppose us." Their trust paid off. The $74,000 that Coburn raised in November and December tripled the rate at which he had been receiving PAC money.

That letter was mild compared with a similar dispatch earlier in the year from DeLay, a no-nonsense missive that helped establish his reputation as the Hammer. Days before freshman Randy Tate of Washington State was to hold a fund-raiser in Washington, D.C., DeLay sent out a letter listing the exact sum each PAC had given to the losing cause of Tate's Democratic opponent in 1994, Mike Kreidler. While he was "surprised to see you opposed Randy Tate," DeLay wrote, "you now have the opportunity to work toward a positive future relationship." The note got more demanding—"your immediate support for Randy Tate is personally important to me and the House Republican leadership team"—before closing with an offer of redemption: "I hope I can count on you being on the winning team."

The aftermath of that letter revealed DeLay's unapologetic mode of operation. A journalist got a copy of it and called DeLay's PAC director, Karl Gallant. Rather than being defensive or trying to rationalize the incident, Gallant asked the reporter where he got the letter. When he was told it came from a lobbyist, Gallant responded, "That tells me it's effective. They want you to write a negative story so we'll back off. You just made my day." DeLay agreed, distributing the article to his colleagues.

"It had great impact. It raised him a bunch of money," DeLay later boasted. Indeed, Tate netted more PAC money—$57,000—in the two weeks after DeLay intervened than he had in the previous five months. "We know who we sent the letters to and who we got checks from," DeLay said.

By the December special election of Republican Tom Campbell of California, DeLay had achieved the touch of easy money. Polls registered growing public distrust of Republicans. Democratic strategists were trying to morph every GOP candidate to Newt Gingrich. The Campbell contest was taking on more importance than just a lone congressional contest: It was being regarded as the first electoral test of the revolution. DeLay agreed to raise funds in the final stretch, sitting down with his PAC list and a telephone in a cubicle at the NRCC office down the street from the Capitol building. When he got up three hours later, he had $60,000 in commitments. Campbell handily won the seat.

Two episodes from Newt Gingrich's past serve as important markers in the story of money and the revolution.

History shows, first, that Gingrich began his career as a profligate revolutionary. Staffers at the NRCC in the 1970s and early 1980s would roll their eyes when the small-college history professor with muttonchop sideburns strolled through the door, knowing they were in for a long day of lectures on the Ming dynasty and

a barrage of expensive ideas for promoting his conservative opportunity society. In those early days, recalled Steve Stockmeyer,
then the executive director of the NRCC, "Newt was very naive
about money. He was always coming up with ideas on how to
spend it, not raise it. He never had the Midas touch, nor did he have
the time. He was not a fund-raiser. He had no idea what things
cost."

History also shows that the more time Gingrich spent watching
the Democrats accumulate power and money during the 1980s,
the more anger welled inside him toward corporate political action committees and the accommodating atmosphere that allowed
them to give so much money to the other side. This frustration
reached the exploding point during a meeting several years ago
in the office of then House Minority Leader Robert Michel of
Illinois. A delegation of PAC lobbyists had requested the session to explain their opposition to a campaign finance reform proposal supported by many Republicans that would have eliminated
PACs altogether. They argued that the Republicans were using
their proposal as a political tool to beat up the Democrats. They
brought along a study defending their giving patterns, showing
that in competitive races the business community supported the
most pro-business candidate of either party. Often that was the
Democrat.

Gingrich entered the meeting in the middle of the argument and
"went through the roof," as one participant recalled. "We got a very
tough tongue-lashing." Another witness remembered that "Newt
was very combative and lectured us for thirty minutes, never letting us have a word. He just wanted to stamp, rant, and rave. He
was making the point that the business community was giving
too much to the Democrats." Gingrich was still venting when the
buzzer signaled a vote on the House floor. The congressmen left
but returned a few minutes later, except Gingrich, who never came
back. When they had settled around the table again, Michel noted
his fiery colleague's absence and said, "Now we can get on with
the meeting."

But despite his early naivete about the ways of money and his later antipathy toward the business world for funding his enemies, Gingrich, more than DeLay or any other figure, was most responsible for turning the revolution into a money machine. As recently as 1993, the financial situation for the Republicans seemed bleak. They were, in the words of Chairman Paxon, "walking in the valley of the shadow of death." Their congressional committee was $4.5 million in debt and they lacked the wherewithal to reverse the situation. They were the minority party in the House and Senate and without the White House.

Paxon, who had been dining with beer lobbyist David Rehr and BellSouth's Dan Mattoon on the night that the NRCC post became open, got their commitments to lead a PAC steering committee responsible for boosting contributions. He moved as quickly to cut costs, trimming the staff from eighty-eight to twenty-six and eliminating expensive consulting contracts. Still, House Republicans entered the 1994 election year in weak financial condition. Their fund-raising relied largely on a direct-mail list that had become utterly obsolete. Of the more than 1 million names on it, only one in ten had given to the party in recent years. Many were in nursing homes or dead.

But if the party seemed equally moribund, Gingrich would not believe it. By April 1994 he had become convinced that the Republicans would seize control of the House that year. He came over to the NRCC and wrote personal appeals for funds claiming that the Republicans would soon be in the majority. When direct-mail experts questioned whether that was overpromising, Gingrich said he would not sign the letters unless they went along with him.

"Gingrich was for my purposes the whole ball game when we wanted to raise money," said Grace Wiegers, then director of fund-raising for the NRCC and later head of Gingrich's leadership PAC, Monday Morning. Along with direct mail, Gingrich persuaded his Republican colleagues that the revolution was at hand, that they could finally take over the House if they worked together to get the money. In August and September 1994 he met individually with more than 150 Republican members, assigning fund-raising tasks and goals to each of them. Incumbents from safe seats were asked to raise $50,000 for Republican challengers or vulnerable colleagues. Ranking minority members of House committees made pledges to Gingrich to raise even larger amounts traveling for other candidates on the road.

When the revolution arrived, Gingrich had a system in place for maintaining and expanding the money operation. DeLay would be his hammer. Paxon would serve as cheerleader. Armey would position himself as ideological arbiter. Boehner would nourish the business coalitions, bringing a dozen of them in for regular Thursday sessions to discuss how the corporate world could advance conservative policy. Committee chairmen Thomas Bliley of Commerce, Bill Archer of Ways and Means, and Bud Shuster of Transportation and Infrastructure would cultivate industries in their turf.

The lines between the elected revolutionaries and their business cohorts occasionally crossed. Lobbyists led by UPS's Paul Smith all but wrote DeLay's regulatory moratorium bill. Congressman Shuster of Pennsylvania raised money for the revolution with the assistance of his former top staffer, Ann Eppard, a transportation lobbyist whose clients included Amtrak, Conrail, Federal Express, and the Pennsylvania Turnpike Authority, all of whom had issues pending before Shuster's committee. Eppard maintained a close political and personal relationship with her old boss. She worked as a paid political consultant for his election campaigns. Shuster occasionally worked at her Potomac waterfront apartment. At the same time that she was soliciting money from industry for the "Bud Shuster Portrait Committee," which hoisted a painting of the chairman in his committee room, she was also sending out fund-raising letters for Republican candidates. One to industry colleagues ended with the assertion: "This dinner is of personal importance to Chairman Shuster."

What the Republicans did in 1995 differed from the old days of Democratic control more in degree than in kind, according to one lobbyist affiliated with the Democrats. "Democrats have not been more ethical, but they tended to be more concerned about their images, because they tended to be a little more responsive to the Naderites and the groups that follow political contributions," the lobbyist noted. "So they tended to be a little more shamed about that sort of thing."

WHAT is Newt doing? That was the reaction back in Washington on June 11, 1995, when the speaker, at an outdoor forum with President Clinton in Claremont, New Hampshire, shook hands on an agreement to form a bipartisan commission on campaign finance reform. The handshake took his allies back in Washington by surprise, and revealed growing tensions within his revolution. At the next meeting of the House leadership, Gingrich was questioned about his deal with the president. The tone of the meeting, said one participant, was "Why the hell did you go and do that?" Armey, responsible for scheduling the revolution's legislative agenda, worried about how he would be able to fit the issue into an already packed calendar. DeLay, and to a lesser degree Paxon, questioned whether the timing was right and whether the Republicans should cede anything to Clinton and the Democrats now that the revolution's money machine was operating so effectively. Gingrich's response was that the handshake "buys us time." He needed to think the issue through.

Another wing of Gingrich's House, represented by Sam Brownback of Kansas and Linda Smith of Washington, along with veteran moderate Christopher Shays of Connecticut, was pushing Gingrich from the other side. If the Republicans did not clean up Washington and prove that they were not continuing business as usual, they said, the revolution would collapse from a fatal flaw of financial excess. If reform did not happen on the Republican watch, said Shays, it would become "our Achilles' heel." While Shays and Brownback took Gingrich's handshake with Clinton as a sign that he supported reform, Smith was skeptical. She said she thought he was just stalling.

Gingrich found himself in a familiar position: on both sides of a debate and looking for another way entirely. He understood the call for reform and had a lingering resentment toward PACs for funding the Democrats during the Coelho era. But he also felt equally strongly that the revolutionaries should not unilaterally disarm themselves while they were engaged in a more profound struggle of what he called the "Information Age." Traditional concepts of power and money were outdated, in his view, and attempts to reform the political system by dealing only with campaign finances were obsolete.

Gingrich believed that the real fight was not over money but information and how it is disseminated. Money was one weapon in that struggle, and important to the movement as a way to counter the American mass media, which the speaker considered largely hostile to the revolution. Gingrich said as little as possible about the issue after the handshake, promising that at some point he would deliver a white paper on the subject. As months went by, the reformers grew increasingly agitated. At Shays's request, Gingrich met with the reformers in his office late one afternoon just before the Columbus Day break. While Shays hoped to discuss another reform issue involving a gift ban, the meeting devolved into a tense confrontation over campaign finance reform between Gingrich and Linda Smith, who had just planted a story with conservative columnist Robert Novak in which she said that the leadership was not telling the truth about their intentions on reform.

The session grew more pointed after Gingrich angrily kicked the staff out of the room. He was feeling overwhelmed by other concerns that day, including Medicare and Bosnia. He was late for a meeting at the White House, and freshman Smith kept jabbing at him. "She was very direct with him. He was very direct with her. Neither of them lost their temper, but both were very forceful," Shays said. "I thought Linda had made her point with one exclamation point. Then two. Then three. Newt was trying to convince her that this was not something he hadn't thought a lot about, because he had." Noting that Smith was working with Common Cause and United We Stand in pushing campaign reform, Gingrich told her that she had to decide whether she wanted to be an outsider or work with the House leadership. "Whatever you decide is okay with me," he said. "We just have to know."

Smith wanted to know why Gingrich needed a commission, why he could not just support legislation eliminating PACs, as he had done when he was in the minority. She told the speaker that he tried to carry too much of the burden himself and that he should let others take the load on this issue.

"Nobody can do it but me! I have the most experience," Gingrich said. "I'm the only one who can do this. I'll just have to take some time this week and write a paper on it."

"Wait a minute, Newt," Smith responded, stunned by the seeming arrogance. "Don't you think the rest of the people in this room have the cumulative brainpower of you?"

Shortly after that meeting, the leadership announced that the House Oversight Committee would hold hearings on campaign finance reform starting November 2 and that Gingrich would be the first to testify. One aide took memos from a group of informal advisers, including Steve Stockmeyer, the former NRCC director who now ran the National Association of Business PACs. Stockmeyer had a study that found PACs were mentioned more negatively in the press than Timothy McVeigh or Mark Fuhrman. There was no way to turn around the public sentiment, he said, but that did not mean that legislators had to follow the crowd. PACs were invented as a reform in the 1970s, he noted, and what reform did away with them would probably create a system that was worse. Senator Mitch McConnell of Kentucky sent a letter over to the House noting that the Republicans had killed campaign finance reform before the 1994 elections—"proof positive that this issue is not a hindrance to us at the polls." In a handwritten P.S., McConnell added: "We'd be foolish to throw away our ability to compete."

Another Gingrich aide began piecing together his speech. He plunged into a long assigned reading list and followed up on the speaker's request to compare the amount of money spent on political campaigns with what is spent on advertising products. Companies spent $100 million selling two stomach acid pills recently, he discovered, one-sixth of the total amount spent on all congressional campaigns in 1994. One of the great myths of American politics, Gingrich concluded, was that campaigns are too expensive. He believed that most of the criticism of the campaign system came from "nonsensical socialist analysis based on hatred of the free enterprise system."

Linda Smith was sitting one row behind Gingrich and off to his right when he delivered those conclusions. She wanted to watch his eyes and his facial expressions as a means of gauging his earnestness, she said, but as he continued to attack the reformers, including some of the groups she had been working with, she became increasingly angry. "His anger at the media drove what he said," she concluded. She retreated to her office, where she reached a final decision on Gingrich's earlier ultimatum to her: She would work from the outside.

GINGRICH'S lieutenants were content with his speech. If reform was inevitable, they felt, it would not involve the elimination of PACs and would not diminish the role of money in the revolution. DeLay said he would not be satisfied until PACs gave an appropriate amount to the Republicans. "Ninety percent would be about right," he declared. DeLay has a running competition with Gingrich over who can raise the most money for his leadership PAC. He trails, and probably always will, but he said he finds inspiration every time he goes out there and talks about the movement and brings in more cash. There are scores of revolutionaries out doing the same thing, but he is not worried that they might trip over each other.

"It's a big country," said the Hammer.

TEN

War of Words

ONE OF NEWT Gingrich's favorite sayings holds that politics is war without blood. In his Third Wave construct, we live in an information age in which the weapons of choice are words and the winners are those who define them, redefine them, test them, deliver them, and repeat them in ways that devastate the opposition or provide the best protection against enemy attack. During the first year of his conservative revolution there was a relentless if often elusive search for the most potent words.

Nowhere was that more evident than in the battle over Medicare, the government-run medical program for elderly Americans. Since its inception in 1965 as part of Lyndon Johnson's Great Society, Medicare had grown so popular that its budget was compared to a "third rail" that would electrocute anyone who touched it. The information war on the issue was unavoidably dangerous and sensitive, one that required extra attention from the speaker and a carefully drawn strategic plan for a long campaign that would take up most of 1995. Gingrich fought for his Medicare proposal with a vast communications army, using polls, focus groups, corporate coalitions, imagemakers, lobbyists, radio talk shows, and the full apparatus of the Republican National Committee and the House Republican Conference. It was a battle, he realized, that might determine the fate of his entire revolution.

The rhetorical planning began one afternoon in March 1995, when Gingrich convened a group to discuss what words should be used in the war. Reflecting his tastes, that initial meeting featured a peculiar blend of public relations jargon and Pentagonese. Among those in attendance were House members from the speaker's Design Group, eight congressmen he had handpicked to draft sensitive Medicare legislation outside normal committee channels. Also on hand were staffers from CommStrat, the communications strategy team of press flacks who would sell the plan, which they called "the product" and handled as an "account."

The speaker's conference room on the second floor of the Capitol was "filled with high anxiety" that day, as one participant said later. Everyone understood the perilous circumstances. The GOP needed to squeeze $270 billion from Medicare to fulfill its promise of a tax cut and balanced budget in seven years, a pledge to which Gingrich had bound his colleagues in February. The odds appeared unfavorable. Medicare was perhaps the most popular social program run by the federal government, and its beneficiaries, 33 million elderly Americans, were a potent political force that even the most zealous conservative budgeteers were reluctant to confront.

Having no history with Medicare, traditionally championed by Democrats, the Republicans would be fighting on enemy turf. They were desperate for a new vocabulary, which is why pollster Linda DiVall was in the room. DiVall, who was both Gingrich's personal pollster and one of a team of consultants aligned with the Republican National Committee, had recently conducted focus groups of senior citizens and baby boomers in several cities to test various rhetorical approaches to Medicare. The results, she said, showed that "language is critically important."

DiVall presented a linguistic paradox: It might be true that the revolution could not prevail without changes in the Medicare system, but if the Republicans were to succeed, revolutionary rhetoric had to be replaced by soothing words that evoked stability. Since seizing control of Congress last November, she warned, Republicans had "created a lot of rhetoric, sometimes too radical." The most sensitive aspect of the operation, the pollster said, would be to "get seniors on board" and make them feel that they had a say in the new-fangled Medicare system while gently moving them toward managed care and health maintenance organizations—a direction that gave Republicans the long-term savings they needed to balance the budget. "Our job," DiVall said, "is to get them to choose the option we want them to choose."

Several words were important to that strategy. "Do not say *changing* Medicare," DiVall stressed. Her research showed that seniors were nervous about change and likely to resist it. At a focus group in Cincinnati on March 6, when seniors were asked what words they preferred, one man offered "preserve." It had a comforting ring to it. DiVall promoted the suggestion of another respondent that they call their legislation "the Medicare Preservation Act." There were other words that should be edited out of the Republican dictionary in discussions of Medicare, DiVall said. She advised the group to be "leery" of the words "cut," "cap," and "freeze"—they would bring nothing but trouble and help Democrats define the process in negative terms.

To underscore "the magnitude of the task" ahead, DiVall showed Gingrich and his team the sardonic answer from a focus group that had been asked to predict the newspaper headline on the day Republican congressional leaders announced they would work on Medicare reform. It read: CONGRESS ENFORCES TERM LIMITS.

DiVall's presentation informed most of the people in the room, but it did little to calm their nerves. Leadership aide Barry Jackson felt as if the entire Republican team was "jumping into the unknown and hoping the ripcords worked." At one point the bell rang signaling a vote on the House floor and all the members left except Gingrich, who rarely votes. He seemed fascinated by DiVall's findings. Alone with the pollster and aides, he became "totally engaged in picking up the nuances." By the time the others returned, he seemed convinced that they could find the right words. The voluble speaker was preparing himself for his version of war.

* * *

THE first word on Medicare already had come from Haley Barbour, chairman of the Republican National Committee (RNC). It was one word that he uttered back in February in four private meetings with Gingrich and John Kasich, and with their counterparts in the Senate, Bob Dole and Pete Domenici.

"Don't," Barbour had said.

A gregarious Mississippian known for his southern aphorisms and colorfully mixed metaphors, Barbour viewed the balanced budget as his party's "soft underbelly" and Medicare as its "Achilles' heel." He urged Gingrich and the others to "take it off the table" for at least two years. Public opinion experts had told him that it took two years to educate and prepare the public for change of that sort. The Democrats wanted the Republicans to go after Medicare "like the Pope hates sin," he said. They had been frustrated when the Republicans declared Social Security off-limits during the 1994 election campaigns and were looking for a chance to push their most potent political issue—the argument that Republicans care more about numbers than people.

Don't touch Medicare for two years, Barbour urged the congressional leaders. They could make up for lost time then, and still reach the seven-year balanced budget goal, by attaining the same amount of savings in five years instead of seven. It was not incidental to Barbour's thinking that a two-year delay would carry the Republicans beyond the 1996 elections. "They all understood that I was right politically. God damn, that ain't rocket science," Barbour recalled. But they rejected his advice. "To a man, they said, if you wait two years, the degree of change required is so much more difficult and drastic than if we start now that it'll end up being much worse."

Once Barbour realized his argument had lost, he became a crucial field general in the rhetorical war, devoting himself and his staff to the Medicare cause. His credo was "Information is our ally." His communications policy, as described by one of his aides, was "to continually flood the faxes, flood the technology, with as much information as you can of what you are doing and why. Fax to the world!" Once you find a theme, Barbour said, "the biggest thing is to get everybody saying the same thing. The only way you can get market penetration is through repetition, repetition, repetition." Over at the RNC headquarters one block from the Capitol, his staff used a more evocative Barbourism: "Repeat it until you vomit."

But there was a problem with the Medicare "account" during those early days of February and March. The public, according to Republican pollsters, did not think there was anything broken in the Medicare system that needed fixing. It appeared that the Republicans were merely tapping into it for their own purposes, to balance the budget and release a similar amount of money for tax cuts for the wealthy. Rank-and-file House members were constantly asking why they had to deal with an issue that they could not easily explain. Gingrich's CommStrat team of press flacks in the Capitol was struggling with the same problem. The speaker kept telling them to "walk people through the moral imperative," but they were uncertain what that meant.

Barbour likened his party's situation to "the country dog that comes to the city: If you stand still, they screw you, and if you run, they bite you on the ass—that's why you've got to be going forward." But he was nervous about going forward without a more compelling theme that could separate Medicare from the numbers game. Linda DiVall's focus groups had started them thinking about what words they should use in talking about Medicare, but they still had no larger rhetorical plan. "We were groping around for a strategy," Barbour recalled.

Then, in the first week of April, the Medicare board of trustees issued its annual report. Word that this document was about to be released had been spreading around Capitol Hill for a few weeks. It was mentioned at a CommStrat meeting, but no one thought it was a big deal. The report came out every year and said essentially the same thing, that Medicare faced long-term financial troubles. No one seemed to pay any attention to it. Barbour had "no idea there was a goddamn Medicare report" until he received a tip from a friendly lobbyist that it would be published earlier than usual. That made him suspicious. "We were out smelling a rat," he said.

"We thought they were going to try to make it look like it was in better condition than it was."

Instead, the report warned that Medicare's trust fund faced bankruptcy by the year 2002. The system's financial condition was deemed "very unfavorable." The report was signed by three cabinet officials in the Clinton administration. Barbour took one look at it and declared, "This is manna from heaven!"

The Republicans had stumbled onto another word they could use effectively in the rhetorical battle over Medicare: "bankruptcy." Barbour carried the news to Gingrich, who considered the report providential. Now they could separate Medicare from the balanced budget. They could say that it needed to be fixed anyway. Gingrich had found his moral framework. The Republicans would repeat it over and over for the rest of the spring and all through the summer. They were saving Medicare from bankruptcy.

Democrats, however, saw a hollow promise in the Republican strategy. The GOP notion of saving Medicare, thought White House aide George Stephanopoulos, "sounded like the old Vietnam argument that they had to destroy the village to save it."

EVERY morning at eight, the press secretaries of CommStrat would participate in a conference call to discuss their message for the day. They would go over what the party office would say in its faxes, what the press secretaries would emphasize in their chats with reporters, what House members on a special Theme Team were planning for the one-minute speeches and longer special orders that begin and end the day on the floor, and what the House Republican Conference was doing to provide cover for members back in their home districts.

It was all part of what Gingrich called the "unified approach" to communications, which gave him tighter control of the message. During his long years as a backbencher when the Democrats controlled Capitol Hill, Gingrich had become obsessed with the power of words and ways of putting out the most effective message. In the early 1980s, although he had minimal status within the Republican rank-and-file, he was the one congressman who would dutifully check in with Ken Duberstein, President Reagan's congressional lobbyist. Duberstein's home phone would ring at six-thirty in the morning or eleven-thirty at night and it would be Gingrich on the line. "What are we doing today?" he would ask. "What's the president's message? How can we coordinate it?"

Now Gingrich operated a seemingly well-oiled message machine that included the CommStrat group, who along with the morning conference calls gathered at least once a week in the speaker's conference room to map out mid-range strategy for the Medicare account. They spent late March and early April following up on DiVall's presentation and trying to compile a group of words that could best impart the Medicare message. They knew that Gingrich was interested in a run of three words. He believed in the rhetorical power of threes, which had biblical connotations. It was Gingrich, after all, who had insisted that the Contract with America be a list of ten, just like the Ten Commandments.

Restructure. Modernize. Transform. Reform. Change. Save. Improve. Protect. Preserve . . . CommStrat members tossed out one word after another and put them together in various combinations in search of the perfect trinity. Bill McInturff, a Republican pollster who along with DiVall was consulting for an RNC-associated think tank, decided to test the words in a poll of four hundred adults age fifty and older. "Restructure" and "modernize" failed to register; they seemed too "techie" and frightening, as did "transform," which was the first choice of only 4 percent. "Change," as DiVall had predicted earlier, was also unpopular, especially among the elderly. Topping the list were "improve" and "protect," at 20 percent each, and "preserve" at 15 percent.

From those findings, McInturff and DiVall wrote a report in which they asserted: "Republicans want to protect, improve and preserve Medicare . . . not transform, reform or change it." They presented their report to Barbour, who practiced saying the words out loud. "This is the last time we're using the old phrases," he said. "Starting today we're going to say this stuff." The next day, Barbour met with Gingrich, who made the final call on the words. There was only one change, the order of the trinity. Walking out of his office with a stack of books under his arm, Gingrich told his communications director, Leigh Ann Metzger, "It'll be preserve, protect, and improve."

Perhaps it was a subconscious rearrangement, for Gingrich never explained it, and neither Barbour nor members of the CommStrat team realized it, but what the speaker had done was make the Republican motto for Medicare strikingly similar to the trilogy in the presidential oath of office, which ends with the phrase: ". . . and will to the best of my ability, preserve, protect, and defend the Constitution of the United States."

On April 24, Barbour sent out a memo to all House and Senate Republicans in which he used "preserve, protect, and improve" seven times in four pages. Four days later, Gingrich delivered his first speech on Medicare in which he emphasized that it was nearing bankruptcy and needed to be "protected and improved." At a press conference on April 30, Dole said the Republicans would "preserve and protect" Medicare and Gingrich declared that "it can be preserved, it can be protected and it can be improved."

The trinity was established. The Republican army was trained and ready to recite it over and over, which they did for a month until further polling brought one additional refinement. In testing the phrase in focus groups in Florida, pollster Frank Luntz discovered that the word "improve" raised expectations beyond what the Republicans intended to deliver. "When seniors hear the words improve and Medicare in the same sentence, they immediately think of lower deductibles, free prescription drugs, subsidized hearing aids . . . and reductions in everything else they now have to pay for," Luntz wrote in a memo to Republicans. He suggested that "improve" be replaced by "strengthen." The change was made official.

* * *

As important to the Republicans as finding the right words was making sure that the press would not use the wrong ones. The ultimate wrong word was "cut." Polls by DiVall showed that the public reacted negatively when told that Republicans would cut Medicare, but positively when informed that spending would increase but at a slower rate. "The phrase 'spending would continue to increase, but at a slower rate' is literally 20% to 40% stronger than 'reduce the rate of growth' and certainly using the word 'cut,' " a DiVall memo said.

House Republicans had already learned a lesson on cuts earlier in the session when Democrats battered them for "cutting" the popular school lunch program. After they lost that message war, when stories had appeared about hungry children and gleeful Democrats had posed for pictures holding ketchup bottles, Republicans vowed from then on they would not allow reductions in the rate of growth to be called "cuts." From Barbour to CommStrat to committee chairmen to House members, the word went out that no statement or story using the word "cut" should go unanswered. "Don't be school-lunched," they warned each other. Barbour promised to raise "unshirted hell" with wayward members of the press.

To reinforce the point at a leadership meeting, Kasich threw a hat on the table and said, "The first guy who says the word 'cuts' has to throw a dollar in the hat." As it turned out, Kasich was the first linguistic perpetrator. "Yeah, I threw in the first buck," he acknowledged later. But he also pounded away fiercely on the issue, calling reporters late at night or early in the morning to warn them off the dreaded word. "I worked them over," he said. Barbour was equally vigilant. He called the anchormen at NBC and ABC and a correspondent at CBS and chided them for using the word. He held breakfasts and lunches with reporters at his conference table at the RNC to go over the difference between cuts and slowing the rate of growth.

Barbour was technically correct. Average spending per Medicare recipient in the Republican plan rose from $4,800 to $6,700 in seven years, numbers that were etched in the mind of every Republican. But when quality of care was factored in, Democrats scored big. To provide today's level of services seven years later would cost $8,000 per beneficiary. And premiums for most pensioners would rise to help generate the huge savings Republicans had envisioned.

There was another lesson that the Republicans took into the Medicare battle from an earlier era. In 1981, Ronald Reagan had suggested that the Social Security system was approaching insolvency and needed restructuring. He was pounded by congressional Democrats and seniors' groups who accused him of cutting Social Security to fund tax cuts for the rich. The reaction was so strong against the plan that Reagan withdrew it within five months and forbade members of his administration from mentioning the words "Social Security" again until the public was ready to accept the findings of a bipartisan commission.

One of the key outside advisers to the CommStrat team this year was Pam Bailey, a health care lobbyist who had been an assistant secretary of public affairs at the Department of Health and Social Services during what she called "the Social Security fiasco of 1981." She warned her friends on the Hill that there were "incredible parallels" between 1981 and 1995, and that only a full-scale rhetorical war of the sort Gingrich was planning could avert a reoccurrence of the earlier disaster. Gingrich himself sought advice from two veterans of the old war, Ken Duberstein and Michael Deaver, Reagan's former communications director. When the Democrats began making the argument that the only reason Republicans were overhauling the Medicare system was to find the money to pay for a tax cut that overwhelmingly favored the wealthy, Deaver advised Gingrich to personalize the issue as much as possible and make it seem that Republicans were acting only because they cared about people.

"We were particularly sensitive to this business about Republicans not caring about people," Deaver said. "In the twenty-two years I was with Reagan, we spent about ninety percent of the time trying to do something about that issue. I've been saying to Newt, 'I don't think we're past that. You've got to be sensitive.' "

* * *

ALL the verbs carefully crafted in Washington were sent out to do battle in the theaters of public opinion, places like the steel towns and dairy farms of northwest Pennsylvania. Republican freshman Phil English won the congressional seat there by fewer than 5,000 votes in 1994, emboldening Democrats and their allies to localize attacks on Medicare. The district, stocked with labor unionists and senior citizens, was formidable terrain for the GOP. But it also represented the kind of challenge Gingrich had in mind when he beefed up the House Republican Conference. Dismissed for years as little more than a social club, the conference began to coordinate Republican positions after Clinton took power. The speaker envisioned an even larger role for it when he reorganized the House upon seizing power. He wanted to centralize communications in an office that would force-feed the message to members, monitor its delivery, and help shield it from enemy attack in the home districts. The new chairman of the conference, John Boehner, became the messenger of the revolution.

Every weapon of rhetorical warfare at Boehner's command was needed in English's district. English was one of fourteen Republicans targeted by the '95 Project, a coalition of labor and consumer groups opposed to the GOP's Medicare plan. In July, an organizer moved to Erie and began lining up seniors to criticize the plan at town meetings and press conferences. A month later, English was the target of a labor-sponsored negative television campaign. And during the Columbus Day recess, just before English was to vote on the plan in the Ways and Means Committee, the '95 Project brought a steamroller to a seniors' center. With a poster-sized picture of English stuck to its side, the vehicle mowed down six gray-wigged mannequins.

Freshmen often buckle under such pressure. But in the hand-to-hand combat over Medicare, English had broad cover from 1010 Longworth Building, headquarters for the conference operation. He learned in its basic training on Medicare to use the soothing words of preserve and protect. He was well armed with sample quotes, talking points, and tactics faxed almost continuously. The conference's intelligence gathering tipped him off days before the steamroller event. A conservative radio talk show host in Erie embraced him, one of 250 radio personalities nationwide cultivated by the conference and sent daily poop sheets and interview offers. On the day of the steamroller, English appeared on Pat Campbell's talk show and denounced the event as an outside influence.

More support in the war of words came from allies in the health industry and conservative senior groups, part of the vast network of lobbyists assembled by the Republican Conference under Boehner. Economic interests have long worked closely with both parties, but not until the new majority rose to power with its antiregulatory agenda had so many corporations and trade associations banded together for as many issues under a single party banner. The Coalition to Save Medicare was one of nine broad-based alliances organized by Boehner. Each coalition had a member in the Thursday Group, the steering committee that Boehner chaired weekly in the Capitol to review legislative strategy. The coalition was his "echo chamber" to spread the message, repeated by lobbyists in Washington and executives or grass-roots memberships back home.

In English's district, the Medicare coalition offered the organizational resources of two powerful groups. The Healthcare Leadership Council, representing pharmaceutical, insurance, and hospital interests, provided vital ground support, rounding up people to attend English's town meetings with scripted talking points and fact sheets to distribute. Air support came from the Seniors Coalition, which included Erie in a $2 million television buy touting the Republican initiative. After viewing the battle for a few weeks, the *Erie Daily Times* sided with English, defending him against '95 Project attacks in an editorial. Sensing how he could turn the attacks to his advantage, English mailed out fund-raising appeals the next day. Within two weeks, by the time the House voted to approve the Medicare legislation, he had received $14,000. An elderly woman enclosed a note with her contribution: "May God Bless you and all good men and women who are trying to turn our wonderful United States around—to balance the budget and still help those in need."

* * *

WHILE English was scrambling to hold his own during the bitter fall in Pennsylvania, there were increasing reasons for Gingrich and his allies to get nervous back in Washington. Democratic efforts to link the $270 billion in Medicare savings to tax cuts for the rich reverberated in national television ads. The juxtaposition of the Medicare savings with $245 billion in promised tax relief made it easier to link the two. The sheer magnitude of the attacks was overwhelming. It was as if everyone who had been shoved aside by the revolution began shouting at once. Many of the toughest ads were launched by organized labor, which had moved beyond criticism of specific Republican proposals, such as the weakening of workplace protections, to broad-gauge opposition. The Columbus Day barrage stung a number of Republicans from labor districts, who brought back stories that the message was turning against them. Polls reflected trouble on a wider scale. In the weeks since the Republicans had released all the specifics of their plan, the public was fast losing faith. Support for Medicare restructuring and the other aspects of GOP social policy was diminishing. The product was hurting the account.

With the first House vote on Medicare approaching, pollster Frank Luntz spent the Friday afternoon of October 6 in his Rosslyn office planning for the focus groups he had arranged for the weekend. He approached the job with foreboding. The message seemed blurred. Luntz hoped that these last focus groups before the vote would reveal the right words to restore the momentum. If he presented the Republican plan in the best possible light to panels of seniors, he thought, they would surely provide the clues. As he thumbed through party documents looking for a good summary, he struck on an idea. Why not present the best Democratic plan in one page and the best Republican plan in one page and see what happens?

At eleven-thirty that night, he produced the fourth and final drafts of two plans. He called the Republican version "Mr. Smith" and the Democratic proposal "Mr. Green." The Mr. Smith script cited the bankruptcy threat and emphasized the long-term solution offered by Republicans. Mr. Green's plan argued that Medicare is not going bankrupt and could be fixed at a cheaper price with no additional premiums or deductibles and no threats that hospitals will close or that certain doctors will be placed off-limits.

The next day, Luntz took the plans to Columbus, Ohio, where he had assembled a dozen people with an average age of sixty-five and no strong political leanings. To Luntz's surprise, everyone preferred Mr. Smith's plan, stressing in different ways that they would accept the personal cost if it brought long-term results. They kept talking about solutions for the next generation. Luntz raised his arms over his head in a Rocky salute, then quickly folded them behind his head to maintain the veneer of objectivity. He knew that he had something that would turn heads in Washington. The polling numbers that had been depressing members the last few weeks now had an antidote, he thought — good communications.

Luntz was so excited he tried to test the findings on the America West flight to Philadelphia, handing out pillows, blankets, and copies of the Smith and Green proposals until a stewardess intervened. His findings began circulating in Washington before the night was over. By Monday afternoon he was in Newt Gingrich's office briefing the speaker and other party leaders. Republicans should take heart, Luntz said. Their plan would be a winner if they emphasized the generational theme. "We sat back for a while and let the Democrats take the high ground morally and emotionally," he said.

Newt Gingrich had a few more words to add to his list. The trilogy of preserve, protect, and strengthen would now be followed by the phrase "for the next generation." Haley Barbour put Luntz's memo and a transcript of the Columbus focus group in his talking points that day for House and Senate members. Rising in the House before the October 19 vote where the House approved his plan, Gingrich repeated the mantra a final time: "We want a solution that preserves and protects Medicare for seniors and that sets the stage for the baby boomers." The bill passed with 231 votes, including all but six members of his own party.

GOP Conference Chairman Boehner had said months earlier that as difficult as it would be to put together a Medicare policy, the communications battle would be ten times tougher. "It still is," he said after the vote, looking ahead to negotiations with the Senate and President Clinton, who had vowed to veto the House plan and fight the Republicans word for word. "Communications is where it's all at. It's not what you're doing but the perceptions that are so important."

At the White House, advisers to President Clinton expressed admiration for Gingrich's communications monolith, marveling at the way the Republicans pressured the news media to stop writing about cuts and how Gingrich was able to draft a plan largely in secret without taking the criticism that Clinton's aides did when they crafted their health package. "Newt's very good," said Stephanopoulos. "He has his word list. But he has a very bad hand." A hand, in fact, that seemed hauntingly similar to the one the Democrats held with health care. It was almost one year earlier that Clinton had dejectedly ended his failed health care campaign. Although his plan extended to everyone and was more prescriptive than the Republican Medicare proposal, there were striking similarities: Both became increasingly hard to explain in simple terms. Both challenged the established systems. Both hoped to save money by encouraging the trend toward health maintenance organizations. And both were carried forward with some measure of arrogance by proponents who thought they were serving noble causes.

AFTER all that intensive planning by Gingrich and his communications team, after a year of focus groups, polls, and constant refinement of message, the Republicans gave the opposition some powerful new ammunition in the war of words even while they were celebrating the successful vote in the House. Appearing before the American Conservative Union on October 24, Bob Dole declared that he was proud to count himself among twelve House members who had voted against the creation of Medicare in 1965 "because we knew it wouldn't work." That same day, in a speech to the Blue Cross/Blue Shield Association, Gingrich said of the Health Care Financing Administration, the agency that runs Medicare: "We don't get rid of it in round one because we don't think that's politically smart. . . . But we believe it's going to wither on the vine because we think people are voluntarily going to leave it."

Within hours, consultants at the Democratic National Committee had drafted a response ad that began: "The Republicans in Congress. They never believed in Medicare and now they want it to wither on the vine." Dole and Gingrich argued that they had been misinterpreted. They said they were speaking out against the overburdening bureaucracy of Medicare, not the program itself. But they were flailing away against perceptions. Once again, rather than finding a rhetorical path out, they had talked their way back into trouble.

The speaker was getting sloppy with his words again. It was a characteristic that his lieutenants had learned was part of the Gingrich package. They would listen to him talk with equal parts awe and apprehension, never sure where his hyperactive mind would take him. Different feelings could send him off in the wrong direction. Sometimes he was too sure of himself. Sometimes he was uncertain and tried too hard to convey a sense of utter conviction. Other times he was tired or angry. But now, for the first time since the glory of the previous winter, Gingrich was showing a larger sense of disarray. He was forgetting some of the lessons he had learned from those thousands of hours he had spent studying how to manage and lead large institutions. For so long he had seemed to be clearheaded about where he wanted to take his troops. He had delegated when he could and asserted control when it was required. This is what we will do this month, he would say, and everyone knew what their responsibilities were. But in October he seemed confused. He was starting to try to do things that in the past he had left to Armey and Boehner and DeLay. He was starting to isolate himself from them and from what had been a unified leadership staff.

Although the leadership remained for the most part united on policy issues, tension was becoming more noticeable even there. It had become apparent to Gingrich and a few other members of his inner circle that the revolution had misjudged its mandate in some areas. Not on the Medicare issue—the conviction and solidarity there were still solid—but more on environmental questions. Week by week, the perception grew stronger within the leadership team that they had blown it on the environment. "We kinda looked up one day and said, 'This wasn't smart,' " recalled Boehner. Gingrich was particularly strong on that point. "Let's stop shooting ourselves in the foot on that one," he told his lieutenants, his words directed most clearly at Tom DeLay, the antiregulatory firebrand. "Those bills aren't going anywhere this year. Let's regroup and get started in a more appropriate way next year."

It was not a full-scale retreat, but it added to an incipient sense of concern. It had been nearly a year since they had taken office with revolutionary fervor, flaunting their power to transform social and economic policy. "Promises made, promises kept," they had declared. But where were the promises now? Parts of Cass Ballenger's massive overhaul of workplace regulations had been imposed through appropriations cutbacks, but the centerpiece legislation never got out of committee. Tom DeLay's moratorium on safety and environmental regulations was stalled in a Senate panel. Bill Goodling, who had reversed a career of moderation to push for the elimination of federal controls on child nutrition programs, had been fighting Senate Republicans for months and was being forced to settle for an experiment involving a handful of states. Although Senate negotiators approved $493 million for the B-2 bomber, they gave Clinton an option, which he would exercise, to buy spare parts, not the new planes sought by B-2 advocates to keep the production line warm. The Senate had still not taken up the House's most sweeping attempt to curtail social service programs, the Labor–Health and Human Services bill.

What was the strategy now? What, the staff wondered, did Gingrich want them to do? One day at a leadership meeting he said that they had to focus more of their message on President Clinton. Clinton was the problem. Clinton wanted the status quo, he said. Clinton liked big government. They had to make the case that Clinton was not defending the people, he was defending the bureaucracy. The communications team went off and spent a week developing a new message directly relating the Medicare and balanced budget issues to Clinton. When they came back to present their ideas to the speaker, Gingrich snapped, "Why are we talking about Bill Clinton? Bill Clinton doesn't matter!" The communications team retreated and drafted a new plan that ignored Clinton. But when they presented it to Gingrich, he had changed again. He was back on a Clinton kick. Pound Clinton, he said. Pound the cabinet secretaries.

Everyone was confused. This was not the way it used to be.

ELEVEN

"Tell Newt to Shut Up!"

ONE DAY IN the middle of September, at the end of a meeting between congressional leaders and White House officials, House Majority Whip Tom DeLay sauntered up to Vice President Al Gore and said: "You have to realize we're serious. We'll shut down the government if we have to to balance the budget."

"Our polls show you guys lose if the government shuts down," Gore responded.

A YEAR had passed since Newt Gingrich swept to the top with a cyclonic force that seemed to suck all the oxygen out of the White House and forced Bill Clinton to utter the inherently humiliating claim that he was still relevant. Now, finally, on the afternoon of Monday, November 13, the moment of confrontation was at hand. When everything was on the line, Gingrich's revolution and Clinton's presidency, who ultimately would prevail?

The government was running out of money. Most of the major annual bills financing the government were still unresolved. If nothing happened before midnight, the federal behemoth would be forced to shut down. Congress had just approved an emergency measure to keep things going for another eighteen days, but in the parlance of the town, it was not a "clean" CR, or continuing resolution. It was loaded with changes in Medicare premiums and education funding that the White House could not accept. Clinton said he would veto it. In a final effort to avert the shutdown, the Republican leadership asked for a meeting at the White House. Some advisers thought Clinton should shun them. Gingrich and his troops were the ones forcing the shutdown, they argued. Let them feel the pain. No, said chief of staff Leon Panetta. "We have to be serious about this. If they want to talk, we should talk."

When the Republican delegation reached the White House, Bob Dole spoke first for his side. He tried to set a reasonable tone. They had reached a serious point, he said, and each side had to consider what it really had to have for an agreement and what the other side had to have. He was trying to open the door to a candid conversation. Gingrich then complained that the White House was making movement toward compromise more difficult by labeling him and his troops "extremists."

"Newt," said Panetta, "you don't come to the table with clean hands."

Armey took up the Republican cause. He said that the Democrats' scare tactics on Medicare and Medicaid had frightened his mother-in-law and her friends. "We could hardly get her into a nursing home, you guys have scared them so much!"

Clinton had remained calm and relatively quiet until then. But he disliked Armey and what he was saying. He said he could not address the specific cases of Armey's mother-in-law and her friends. "But let me tell you there are a lot of older women who are going to do pretty darn bad under your budget," Clinton said.

"I'm sorry if you feel that way," the president went on. "But let me tell you, you're not going to get much pity from me. I sat there and watched all you guys talk about how our deficit reduction plan would kill the economy. And it didn't. And how our health care plan was bureaucratic. And it wasn't. So don't look for any pity from me. I want to make one thing clear. I am not going to agree to your Medicaid package no matter what. I am not going to agree to education cuts. If you want to pass your budget, you're going to have to put somebody else in this chair. I don't care what happens. I don't care if it all comes down around me. I don't care if I go to five percent in the polls. I am not going to sign your budget. It is wrong. It is wrong for the country."

There were different reactions to Clinton's emotional statement. His aides were proud—and surprised by his show of strength. They had been afraid that he would cave. Gingrich seemed a bit stunned, and reverted to Dole's approach of seeking common ground. He softened his voice and talked in conciliatory tones about how both he and the president had problems with the Congressional Budget Office (CBO) and the way it estimated budget numbers. He said he understood that there would have to be more compromises, that Clinton would not sign a bill that did not fund his national service program and other programs important to him.

Armey was unmoved, and seemed alarmed by Gingrich's conciliatory tone. Clinton's speech, he said, did not impress him one bit. He complained again about having to "listen to all these lies" by the White House mischaracterizing the Republican leaders and their budget.

"Mr. Armey," Clinton responded, "at least I never, ever have and never expect to criticize your wife or any member of your family."

Gingrich tried again to make the dialogue less pointed, but by then it was obvious that there would be no resolution. At midnight, the government would shut down. When the Republican contingent left the White House, Vice President Gore and other staff members congratulated Clinton.

"Mr. President, I've heard you say that before and it really sounds great," Gore said of Clinton's damn-the-consequences speech to Armey. "You should say that to the American public. It's very moving for people to hear that you're willing to lose this election for what you believe in. Just one little thing: When you said you didn't care if your popularity goes down to five percent, you wouldn't sign the bill. I think it would sound a little better if you said, 'I don't care if my popularity goes down to zero.'"

Clinton put an arm around Gore. "No, that's not right, Al," he said. "If I go down to four percent, I'm caving."

There had not been that kind of laughter in the Oval Office in a long time, the loud guffaws of winners who can afford to seem self-effacing.

FOR months Washington had been obsessed with the notion of a train wreck coming down the line: Gingrich and his budget-cutting revolutionaries steaming in from one direction. Clinton and his veto rolling in from the other. Perhaps the fact that it was so visible for so long made few people believe that it would actually happen in the end. Certainly one side would stop, or both would move off to a track of compromise. But the train wreck did happen. Many times, in fact. A series of train wrecks began that day in mid-November and continued into the first two weeks of 1996. There was debris everywhere. The personal casualties included hundreds of thousands of federal workers who lost time and money, and a larger number of citizens who missed the services of their government.

Among the political casualties, Gingrich was perhaps the most seriously wounded. His own troops, including members of his leadership team, thought he was losing control, and they were frustrated by a string of comments he made that seemed self-destructive. "He picked the wrong bloody moment to take out a .357 and shoot both kneecaps off," one said. Gingrich's internal position in the House was further weakened by his efforts to maintain a unified front with Senate Majority Leader Dole, who House members felt was too accommodating. And Gingrich's self-confidence was eroded when he finally tried to negotiate a budget deal himself, a task at which he proved inept, his trips to the White House ending in confusion and dismay as time after time he was seduced by Clinton and the atmosphere in the Oval Office. But of all the major players in the end game, Gingrich was also in the most difficult situation, constantly trying to balance the competing pressures he felt from his troops, from Dole and the Senate, and from the White House.

He was often astute at anticipating the consequences of various courses of action, but less adept at shaping events. On the shutdown, his missteps had so weakened him in the public eye and within his rank-and-file that he was not in a good position to overcome members of his leadership team who pushed hardest to close the government, a policy that Gingrich privately opposed. On the budget negotiations, he had become convinced early on that the White House wanted a deal, and was so taken by Clinton every time he encountered him that he shaped all of his strategies around that notion. It took him a long time before he would finally decide otherwise.

Bob Dole's role during the end game was the most intriguing and least understood. At times, especially during arguments about the shutdown, he appeared to be closer to the White House than to Gingrich and the House. But Dole, in his terse, close-to-the-vest style, was playing a careful game. On the one hand, he wanted to get rid of the shutdown problem so that he could go campaign for president. On the other hand, even as he angered some of the true believers in the House, he was careful not to sever his close relationship with Gingrich, who he thought was important to him both as a symbol of the young, activist wing of the party and as the only person, despite his troubles, who could move the House. Many strategists at the White House presumed that Dole would be the least interested in achieving a balanced budget agreement, since the lack of a deal might serve as a campaign issue for him. Dole's actions in working toward a deal were more complicated. While constantly pushing Gingrich and others to keep returning to the bargaining table, he was also at times the most pessimistic that an agreement ultimately could be struck.

President Clinton, like his staff, was divided from the start. On one side was consultant Dick Morris, who had spent the year successfully helping Clinton reconstruct his image as a centrist and who believed that a budget deal was an important final step in that process. The complication with Morris was that he also believed that Gingrich and the House Republicans had placed themselves in an impossible situation by cutting Medicare and demanding a balanced budget in seven years, and that they were merely looking for a graceful way to surrender. Morris had tantalized Clinton with the prospect that he had already won even before the first train wreck occurred.

On the other side, taking a hard-line position, was a larger group of Clinton advisers, led by Treasury Secretary Robert Rubin and senior White House aide George Stephanopoulos, who maintained that Clinton should not compromise too much in search of a deal and needed to maintain a clear distinction between his position and the Republicans on four key issues: Medicare, Medicaid, education, and the environment.

Just as the Republican position was shaped in part by Gingrich's personality and petty reactions to perceived slights, the Democratic side was changed by Clinton's personality and one of his apparent misstatements. The triangulation theory that Morris had designed for him, in which he would set himself up as the voice of reason between Gingrich's revolutionaries and liberal Democrats in Congress, was rearranged from the moment in early fall when he declared at a Houston fund-raiser that he regretted some of the tax hikes he inspired in 1993. That statement so infuriated Democrats in Congress that Clinton from then on became more solicitous of them.

The Houston statement ended up having an ironic effect. It hurt Clinton in the short run with Democrats in Congress who were already furious with the White House because of Morris's triangulation theory. But it stiffened the president's resolve, helping him forge a new bond with congressional Democrats while at the same time leading Republicans to the deceptive conclusion that he was a vacillator who would inevitably cave on the budget. It also gave new leverage to members of Clinton's staff who opposed a deal, and made it harder for Republicans to read and predict the president's actions. Gingrich believed throughout December that Clinton would abandon the liberals and strike a deal. It was one of many ways the speaker would guess wrong.

* * *

Two days after the shutdown began, at a breakfast with reporters, Gingrich lost his cool. It was a calculated explosion; he had told his chief of staff that he was going to speak his mind. But it certainly had results beyond his calculations. Clinton had forced the shutdown, by the way he had treated the Republican leaders, he told the reporters. He was especially irritated by the way the president snubbed them on the plane ride to Israel and back for Rabin's funeral. "This is petty. But you land at Andrews Air Force Base and you've been on the plane for twenty-five hours and nobody has talked to you and they ask you to get off the plane by the back ramp," Gingrich said. "You just wonder: Where is their sense of manners? Where is their sense of courtesy?" His anger over that treatment, Gingrich said, was one reason why the continuing resolution that Clinton had vetoed on Monday night was so loaded with provisions the White House disliked. "It's petty," he said. "But I think it's human."

Even as he was talking, Gingrich realized that he was making a mistake. He could not control himself. He blurted out that his press secretary, Tony Blankley, who was pacing back and forth in the rear of the room, would certainly be uneasy about what he was saying and the way he was saying it.

It was not just Blankley, as it turned out, but the entire Republican rank-and-file and the American public. Gingrich thought he was giving a technical explanation of what had gone wrong in the negotiations. He offered his analysis of the plane trip as evidence that the White House had made a strategic decision not to move on the negotiations. That turned out to be the right analysis—the White House had indeed decided not to move any further. But the analysis was overwhelmed by the melodrama of the moment. Gingrich sounded like a whiner, a little boy who behaved irresponsibly when he didn't get his way. That became his image. He was lampooned in cartoons and columns and radio shows across the nation.

The embarrassment intensified when the White House released a photograph taken inside Air Force One that clearly showed Clinton and his staff talking with Gingrich and Dole. It did not matter that the picture captured a quick meeting at which the congressional delegation was being briefed on the funeral. Gingrich had been had. His popularity in public surveys, which had been dropping steadily all year, plummeted further.

BY the Sunday afternoon of November 19 the government had been shut down for six days. Negotiations between Congress and the White House had stalled and now were being conducted with the electronic remoteness of letters faxed back and forth between Bob Dole's office and Leon Panetta's office. In style though certainly not in gravity, it was almost like the Russians and Americans during the Cuban missile crisis, some aides thought—words heading back and forth with little explication of what they meant. The fax traffic grew particularly heavy on Sunday, a day when so little was expected to happen that Dan Meyer, Gingrich's chief of staff, brought his youngest son to the office with him.

It was Bob Dole who had forced his side back into action the night before, when he had returned from a campaign trip to Florida and said the Republicans had to make some effort to reopen the government. "We have to at least make an offer so we don't look intransigent," he said. John Kasich, the House budget chairman, agreed with him. Kasich had a sense that the Democrats were starting to break and ready to deal. It was getting close to the point, he thought, that enough Democrats might go along with them to override the president's veto. That had to be why Panetta chased after him so hard, out of breath, his hair flying, the other day outside the House gym, urging another round of talks.

So the faxes began. The Republicans drafted language that reopened the government for a month on condition that the Democrats would negotiate a balanced budget agreement that eliminated the deficit in seven years as scored by the conservative economic estimates of the Congressional Budget Office. The White House attached language saying any agreement would also protect the president's priorities on Medicare, Medicaid, education, and the environment. After rounds of rewriting on each side, with little actual discussion about the precise meaning of the phrases, the proposal had reached a condition where people on each side thought they had a winning deal.

When the fax protecting the president's programs came back okayed by the Republicans, Panetta and Stephanopoulos, the key day-to-day White House strategists, shouted with delight. "Yes!" said Stephanopoulos. "This is it!" said Panetta.

There were a few skeptics on the White House team who thought they might have trouble later with the language. Would they have to present a seven-year balanced budget plan first, or just end up with one at the end? Were the president's priorities equal in the resolution to the pledge on a seven-year balanced budget? When the fax was shown to Clinton, he shared some of those reservations. But Panetta and Stephanopoulos were adamant. They rushed up to Capitol Hill to talk with the Democratic leadership and called back even more enthusiastic. Everyone was on board, they said. Go with it. Clinton agreed.

In Dole's office, there was an equal degree of excitement. When the fax came across with the White House accepting their language on a seven-year balanced budget scored by CBO, Kasich turned to Senate Budget Chairman Pete Domenici and slapped him a high-five. There had been some disagreement among the Republicans on how and whether to deal with the White House. Republican National Committtee Chairman Haley Barbour had been arguing for months that they should force the president's hand and never assume that he would compromise until public opinion made him. But Barbour's influence in the negotiations was diminishing. Throughout the summer and early fall, he had been invited to attend the daily strategy sessions between Dole and Gingrich and serve as a facilitator of sorts. Dole and his aides eventually concluded that Barbour was shifting the balance of power over to the House by agreeing more often with their position. One day Dole passed the word that Barbour was no longer needed, and he stopped coming. His advice, as it turned out, would be missed.

Some other House members welcomed the November shutdown

and confrontation. They had heard the buzz that Clinton's poll numbers were starting to drop. Let him stew, they said. After all, they had done enough suffering of their own recently. First they had blundered by attaching a Medicare provision to the interim spending measure Clinton had vetoed, allowing him to pound them with his most effective message. Then, on November 15, Gingrich had issued his diatribe about being snubbed on Air Force One, making it look like the shutdown arose from an infantile tantrum. It was, some argued, time to take the offensive. John Boehner believed the shutdown confrontation was bound to happen eventually so it might as well be played out now.

But Kasich, whose interests rested in balancing the budget, not in gaining political points, had thought the time was right for a deal. And he had Dole and Domenici on his side. Gingrich had been a bit more skeptical but willing to give it a try. And now as they all looked at the wording on the latest fax, they felt it was a clear victory for their side. Kasich and Domenici were delighted to see that the White House had capitulated to their demand for a budget proposal scored by the CBO. Before that, the administration had fought being pinned down to seven years, and it had wanted to use rosier projections from the Office of Management and Budget (OMB), providing hundreds of billions more dollars and thus requiring smaller cuts. The Republican team paid little attention to the language the White House insisted on adding to the agreement about how any budget deal would also protect the president's priorities. Gingrich's people considered it nothing more than "hortatory language."

The optimism lasted until morning. All the euphoria of the day before had been premature. They had assumed that the media would treat the deal as a clear win for the Republicans. Instead, the press accepted the argument of White House aides, who had been spinning their side of the story all through the previous night. It was a draw, they had said. Both sides got what they needed. And so it was portrayed in the morning.

A sudden gloom enveloped the speaker's suite on the second floor of the Capitol. Tony Blankley fell into a depression. The press secretary usually displayed more equanimity than his boss when it came to treatment by the media, but this was too much for him to take. The White House had not just won the battle of the morning papers, it was already redefining the agreement on the morning television shows. Panetta described it as a victory for the White House. The agreement, he said, did not necessarily bind them to seven years, nor to CBO scoring, but only to the notion that those factors would be considered in balance with the need to maintain Clinton's budget priorities. Maybe it would take eight years. Panetta and other White House aides understood immediately that the fight from then on would be over the definition of the continuing resolution.

Gingrich and his troops were stunned. They had been naive. The language that seemed superfluous to them was being used by the Democrats to regain control of the message.

HOUSE Republicans returned from the Thanksgiving recess with a common refrain. Their constituents, they said, were telling them to hang tough on the balanced budget. And they were also passing the word along about the leader of the revolution: "Tell Newt to shut up!" The whining over the airplane ride had taken Gingrich's negative ratings over the edge. He might have been the first Speaker of the House who registered on the public scale of recognition, but he was becoming more notorious than famous. The book deal. The Hillary's-a-bitch flap involving his mother. The utility-of-orphanages rap. The accusations about drug use in the White House. The "wither on the vine" line in his Medicare speech. The linking of a brutal murder in Chicago to the decline of the welfare state. All controversial — and now this, the easiest of them all to ridicule. "Tell Newt to shut up!" It wasn't the first time Republican congressmen were hearing it from Republican constituents, but now they were saying it everywhere: at town hall meetings, in the grocery store, at business coalition gatherings, at church. It had reached the point where someone had to say something to him.

Boehner was asked by a number of colleagues to intercede. That was his job. He was the steady Eddie of the leadership team, a deep-voiced, tan midwesterner who trawled the House domain with the loose gait of a high school jock. His demeanor seemed as unruffled as his pin-striped suits. If Gingrich needed to be redressed, Boehner was most likely the one to do it. He raised the latest Gingrich embarrassment at a leadership meeting. It was point six of his regular communications report: "Tell Newt no more stories about airplanes!"

Gingrich did not laugh. Fifteen minutes later, steaming, he turned his head slowly around the conference table. Others in the room knew what was coming. When Newt turned his head like that it reminded some of them of the Terminator movies. You could feel the infrared, they said, and tell that someone was about to get his head taken off. Gingrich rotated his big round head, stared at Boehner, and uttered a line that was as hostile in intent as it was prosaic in wording: "No more stories about the airplane, right?"

But another Gingrich matter that week was even more troubling to Republican members of the House. On the first day back they had heard him suggest, after a meeting at the White House, that he might support Clinton's decision to send troops to Bosnia. He talked about the long Republican tradition of supporting the commander in chief and trying to be helpful on issues beyond the nation's borders "unless you absolutely can't do it." His old friend Bob Walker visited him privately and expressed his grave concern. The Republican House was solidly against Clinton's Bosnia policy, Walker warned. Gingrich was already on thin ice, and this might crack it.

Then Boehner arrived with an even tougher message. Like the other members of the House leadership team, Boehner had enormous respect for Gingrich as the father of the revolution. He considered the speaker the smartest of the group and the only one who could lead them. Yet there was also a measure of caution in the relationship. True conservatives like Boehner and DeLay—even Armey—did not consider Gingrich one of them. He was a radical, a reformer, a doer, but not a true conservative. That sometimes made him unpredictable. Every true conservative in Washington had shared that little secret about Gingrich. It had never seemed a problem until now.

All day long Republican members of the House had been coming up to Boehner and asking about the speaker's position on Bosnia. On Tuesday night, November 28, Boehner finally paid a visit to Gingrich in his office.

"I hate to do this to you," Boehner began. He realized that Gingrich was already feeling low after a miserable Thanksgiving break that had shaken his confidence. "You already have an image problem with the airplane," Boehner continued, "and now this thing with Bosnia. It's probably going to be the straw that breaks the camel's back. There are people out there wanting to question whether you ought to be speaker."

It was, Boehner thought, the toughest thing he had had to do all year, like punching a friend in the stomach.

Gingrich took a deep breath. "What do you think I should do?" he asked.

"Lay low," Boehner said. "And for God's sakes, when it comes to Bosnia, just don't say anything."

"Well, I don't know," Gingrich responded defensively. "If I just say what I've said . . ."

"No, Newt. Stop! Don't say anything."

Gingrich finally accepted the advice. He said nothing more about Bosnia for several weeks.

THAT was the same day budget negotiations started between the White House and Congress down in the Mansfield Room of the Capitol, a windowless, wood-paneled chamber that had the feel of an old gentlemen's club. The budget committee chairmen, John Kasich in the House and Pete Domenici in the Senate, led the Republican team, while Leon Panetta and OMB director Alice Rivlin led the White House contingent.

The Democrats arrived with a larger squad, so there was a debate at first about how many people could be on each side. The Democrats explained why they needed a tableful of congressmen there by evoking the famous Andrews Air Force Base budget deal of 1990, where President Bush infamously retreated from his "No New Taxes" pledge and thereby disheartened the Republicans in Congress. The lesson of Andrews, Panetta argued, was that the table was too small. The session immediately degenerated into an argument over the November 20 continuing resolution that had reopened the government, and sent the two sides back to the negotiating table in search of a budget that could both be balanced and maintain Clinton's priorities.

"You're slashing programs for people! You don't care!" Panetta shouted, rejecting attempts by Kasich and Domenici to get him to present a proposal scored by the CBO that would balance the budget in seven years. Panetta wanted only to talk about programs, not overall numbers.

"Leon, you're never going to get anywhere if you yell like that," said Dick Armey.

"Don't worry, that's just Leon," said Kasich, who was familiar with Panetta's temper going back to the days when he served as chairman of the committee Kasich now ran. "Leon," Kasich continued, "are you saying you're not for a seven-year balanced budget?"

Panetta shook his head no, as did George Stephanopoulos, sitting behind him.

"Well," Kasich continued, "can you produce a seven-year balanced budget that meets your priorities?"

Panetta paused before answering, "Yes, I can."

"When you do," Kasich said, "I'd like to see it."

TWO weeks later, early on the morning of Friday, December 15, Kasich bolted into Gingrich's office with disheartening news. He had been pacing the corridors of the Capitol burning off nervous energy, he said, and upon entering the Rotunda had bumped into Charlie Stenholm, a conservative congressman from West Texas who sat with the Democrats in the balanced budget negotiations and was known to blab.

"What do you know, Charlie?" Kasich asked him, wondering if Stenholm had inside information on a balanced budget proposal that the White House was finally supposed to put on the table that day after two weeks of fruitless negotiations.

"You'll get three-quarters of a loaf at best, and that's being charitable," Stenholm revealed.

This intelligence report enraged Gingrich. He was facing deadline pressure: The federal government would shut down again at midnight unless Congress passed another temporary spending bill, something many revolutionaries in the House were disinclined to do unless they saw substantial progress in the negotiations. And Gingrich also felt deceived. For weeks he had been receiving backchannel assurances that President Clinton wanted a budget agreement and was ready to deal. Clinton had said as much himself in telephone conversations with Dole. Anticipating a serious offer from the other side, congressional Republicans had drafted a new proposal of their own, adding $135 billion to their previous seven-year budget based on more optimistic projections from the Congressional Budget Office.

"Well, then, we're not exchanging offers! We're not!" Gingrich fumed as he and Kasich and their staffs prepared to walk over to Dole's office for a strategy session of what was known as the Big Four (the fourth being Senate Budget Chairman Pete Domenici) before the budget talks.

Once Gingrich reached Dole's office, his anger slowly subsided. The laconic elder statesman from Kansas had a calming effect on the voluble speaker. "What's the problem around here? If we stop being so paranoid and get in the room, we'll probably get going," Dole interjected at one point as the others debated whether they should go forward with the exchange of plans. Then he added dryly: "We wouldn't even be having this discussion if Kasich hadn't run into Stenholm."

That ended the argument. The negotiating team, carrying their latest proposal in a bright red folder, walked across the hall for the start of negotiations. With every step, they were moving closer to chaos and frustration.

The biggest political train wreck of the year happened that day. Budget talks fell apart and a twenty-one-day partial government shutdown ensued. In the larger saga of the budget battle between the Republican Congress and the Clinton White House, no period was more decisive than the weeklong stretch starting that Friday. It was during that period that the public focus shifted sharply away from what the Republicans desired: from who could balance the budget to who was responsible for the government shutdown.

That week also revealed the contrasting leadership styles of Gingrich and Dole, and the limits that each of them faced. Opposite personalities inextricably linked by need and circumstance, the two men found themselves caught between an administration they did not trust and a House rank-and-file they could no longer control. Gingrich, a leader known for his air of certitude, if not arrogance, seemed at times dazed and confused. His House was torn by dissension. There was growing animosity toward the Senate. And while Clinton sent out an array of conflicting signals, his political agents always seemed to be one step ahead.

THE budget-exchange meeting had begun at 11:30 A.M. on December 15, with Panetta, lead negotiator for the Democrats, suggesting that they flip to see which side went first. Alice Rivlin cupped a coin in both hands, shook twice, and dropped it on the table. Kasich called "Heads" and won. The Republicans elected to receive. While passing out a few summary sheets, White House officials began describing their plan. It took Kasich and Domenici "about ten seconds" to realize that Charlie Stenholm was indeed being charitable.

"This is not a proposal," Kasich muttered to a leadership aide. "This is something you could put together in five minutes." He kept his eyes trained on Panetta and Rivlin, who had reputations as deficit hawks, to see if they could talk about it while keeping straight faces. The Democrats offered no movement on Medicare or Medicaid, and few cuts elsewhere. Almost all of their proposed changes were based on reconfiguring the economic assumptions.

Their numbers were still not scored by the Congressional Budget Office.

When Kasich and Domenici pointed that out, Panetta argued that "the CBO is just wrong!" in its conservative economic projections. "We're not going to let you savage our priorities," he said. The Republicans grew quieter and more dismayed. They had no heart for the endeavor when their turn came to present their new proposal.

On the other side, the Democrats and their aides could see that the Republicans were ready to push from the table. Panetta had arrived with a second plan in his pocket, but he never pulled it out. Before they had left the White House that morning, Panetta's team had decided that if the Republicans were desperate to talk, they would take the first plan. There was maybe a 5 percent chance of that, they thought. If the Republicans wanted to blow up the talks, that was their problem.

The meeting was set up with a halftime so both sides could discuss the counteroffers in private before moving ahead. Before they broke up, Panetta asked, "Do you know if anything is going to happen on a CR?"

"I don't know," said Domenici, "I'm not hopeful."

Kasich and Domenici then left for Dole's office.

"Chickenshit!" Domenici shouted as he entered the room. "That was an absolute insult!"

His aide, Bill Hoagland, who had been the most optimistic about the meeting, encountered Gingrich and said, "Mr. Speaker, I apologize. I thought they would come in with more than this today."

Dole moseyed in from a back room.

"You boys settle everything?" he asked, barely showing a smile.

"This is an insult. It's terrible," Kasich muttered. Someone handed Dole the White House summary sheet.

"They've got a paper that shows them [getting] to [a] balanced [budget], right?" he said. This time it was a bit easier to read his sarcasm.

"What do you expect from those guys," Gingrich said. "This is how they've treated us all along."

Dole showed no anger, just exasperation. He was the senior

partner. He had been pushing for a continuing resolution. He had done the most talking with Clinton and seemed the most inclined to take him at his word. Someone suggested that Dole call Clinton right there and complain. That notion was rejected. Kasich and Domenici would go back to the room and deliver the message to Panetta. But what should they do about the CR? Kasich argued that they should keep the government open at least through Christmas. "They'll say it's the Gingrich who stole Christmas if we close it down," he said. Gingrich was thinking the same way. Dole had always been against closing the government, as had Domenici. They would push for a short-term CR.

After halftime, back in the negotiating room, Domenici was restrained and polite. "Thanks for your offer but it doesn't get us anywhere," he said.

Panetta argued that both sides had moved a little. That comment bemused Kasich, who recalled a decisive moment in the first negotiating session nearly three weeks earlier. "Leon, you promised you could do a CBO-scored balanced budget and do it in seven years," he said.

"I never said we could do it with CBO numbers," Panetta replied, waving off a key element of the November 19 agreement between Clinton and the Republicans ending the first government shutdown.

Kasich was flabbergasted, but Domenici did the talking. "We're out of here," he muttered.

Panetta inquired one more time about a continuing resolution. There was no response.

As Panetta, flanked by White House staffers, walked down the corridor after the meeting, he encountered Republican Senator Alan Simpson of Wyoming, who seemed bewildered. The "crazies" in the House had taken over, Simpson muttered.

GINGRICH arrived back on the House side of the Capitol at 3:30 P.M., just as his House leadership team was convening. On the way into the meeting room, H-227, he was introduced to ten parochial school children from upstate New York decked out in plaid uniforms with white shirts. "Want to see my dinosaur?" he asked them, pointing up the hallway to his favorite room in his second-floor office suite, known as the Dinosaur Room because of the glass-encased jaw of a tyrannosaur near its entrance.

Before they could respond, he stepped inside H-227 and faced a somewhat less appreciative audience. The room was buzzing. Some members of the leadership were angry that they had not yet seen the Republican budget proposal that Kasich and Domenici had presented to Panetta. What had they given away? Was it true that they were putting money back into Medicare and welfare? Even DeLay and Boehner had only a glimpse of what was in the proposal. How could they tell members what to say about it if they were ignorant themselves?

One by one, members started to raise questions about a continuing resolution to keep the government open. Don't even try it, they told Gingrich. It will go down in flames. Kasich walked into the room late and was stunned by the atmosphere. "My God," he thought to himself, "they're burning the furniture and they've killed the fatted calf!"

Gingrich, who had been so angry at the start of the day, now seemed tame in comparison to his colleagues. After broaching the subject of the continuing resolution, as the Big Four had agreed on, he listened to the rebukes from his leadership team. Finally he realized that there was no way he could get one through his House. He turned to Dan Meyer and whispered, "Better get Dole. He oughta hear this."

Meyer called Sheila Burke, Dole's chief of staff, and a few minutes later Dole and Burke arrived at H-227. Burke, standing against the wall, rolled her eyes at a leadership aide and whispered, "We're very happy to be here," meaning her boss was a bit grumpy on the walk over.

"I appreciate you coming over, Bob. I just wanted you to listen to what some of our people have to say." He went around the room and called on members to give their assessment for Dole. One by one they attacked the notion of another CR.

The room was wall-to-wall revolutionaries. Senate Majority

Whip Trent Lott slipped in, as did Michigan Governor John Engler, eager to join in the rabblerousing. Kasich caught sight of Engler, occasionally mentioned as a vice-presidential choice for Dole, and joked, "He's off the ticket right there."

At one point there was a knock on the door and in walked a man dressed as Santa Claus. "Ho, ho, ho, I've got a candy cane for you, Mr. Dole," he said. "And I've got one for you, Mr. Speaker!"

Kasich looked over at Sheila Burke, who again rolled her eyes to the ceiling. If Dole didn't already think he was in fantasyland, that clinched it. Then the speeches began again. Dole listened patiently to impassioned House members while softly popping his lips under his breath, "mumumumumom."

"I understand," he finally said. "My question is: What's the end game? Shut down the government and that's the whole story. We don't win."

When one congressman said the press was going to write negative stories about the Republicans no matter what they did, Dole responded: "I'm not worried about the press. I'm worried about the public perception out there. We've got to find some way to turn that around—that we're the ones shutting down government."

But no one in the room was in a mood for that argument. The message was clear. The House was ready to shut it down.

"Thanks a lot for coming over," Gingrich said to Dole at the end.

"You bet," Dole said. "Kinda reminded me of my days in the House over here."

THE leadership meeting was merely a warmup for what was to come. Waiting over in the Ways and Means Hearing Room in the Longworth Office Building was the rest of the House Republican membership. There was no need to poll the rank-and-file on whether there should be a continuing resolution. Gingrich already knew the idea was dead, at least for that day. And the full conference of Republicans was in even more of a lather than the leadership.

The seemingly meager Democratic budget proposal was not the

only thing riling the crowd. Word had come over from the Republican National Committee that the Democrats had purchased large swatches of television time Thursday night, to begin running negative ads against the congressional Republicans starting Friday. This was taken as a cynical maneuver—proof, it was argued, that the Democrats' negotiating offer that morning was a sham. Copies of the ad's text were distributed at the conference. But not all of the anger was directed at the Democrats. Gingrich introduced Kasich to explain the revised GOP proposal. When he noted that more money had been set aside for welfare, some members hissed and booed. "The natives were very restless about that," Kasich said later.

At 5:30 P.M. the staff rolled in a few bulky televisions on carts and plugged them in so the members could watch President Clinton, who was appearing live at the White House press room to talk about the breakdown in the budget talks. Members gasped in disbelief and awe when Clinton placed the blame for the breakdown on the Republicans and said they would be held responsible for shutting down the government again. Chris Shays of Connecticut, holding a portable phone, had to restrain himself from throwing it at the TV set.

After the conference, Gingrich retreated to his office with Kasich, Boehner, Armey, and a few aides. They stayed up late eating fried chicken and goo-goo clusters and talking about the tumultuous day. Gingrich was overcome by a sense that he had been gamed by the Democrats. He was convinced that they had never intended to come in with a serious proposal. And he was awed by the tactical brilliance of the White House, sending Clinton out before the cameras at five-thirty to ensure that his message would be the central one on the evening news shows. The Democrats were better at it, the group agreed. They had been at it longer. They were clever.

"I'm operating on my ex-wife's favorite saying—'Time wounds all heels,' " said Armey. It was just like the old country song, he added: " 'You were only foolin' while I was fallin' in love.' " But the mood was not light. Gingrich was trying to toughen himself for what would be a longer fight than he had anticipated.

"Every meeting we go into with Democrats now we should go in and say, 'We need this,' " he said. "We should never again talk in terms of trust. We should never talk in terms of working coopera- tively." In the coming days, he would learn that that was easier said than done, and he would become the person least able to follow his own hard line. But his optimism was fading. He had problems everywhere, on his left and right, with his own troops and with the White House. He did not sleep well that night, thinking until dawn about how to find a way out.

WHEN a one-page memo fell into their hands on Saturday morning, aides to Tom DeLay reached a swift assessment. Their boss was not going to like this.

Fresh off the laser printer and dated that morning, December 16, the memo was from Newt Gingrich to Republican leaders. It presented a list of assumptions and strategies that Gingrich had developed late the night before, after the balanced budget talks had broken down, and on his way to work that morning, the first day of the second partial shutdown of the federal government.

In bold type across the top, the Gingrich memo declared:

The White House has crossed the line. We want them to understand that if they want a long-term stand-off, we are prepared to stay the course for as long as it takes.

It then listed three assumptions:

- The White House is prepared for a situation in which there is no deal.
- The White House believes they can beat us in a short-term tactical confrontation.
- The White House wants a situation in which they can con- tinue to portray us as extremists. They want to blame the government shutdown on us as irresponsible partisans.

So far, no problems for the DeLay operators, who were, like their boss, firm believers in hardball politics. But what came next they found troublesome. Under his list of strategies, Gingrich proposed passing a continuing resolution through the House on Monday allowing federal employees to be paid through January 3, 1996, then to follow that up with a series of bills to reopen the government but only fund programs that the Republicans supported. After the paroxysms of the previous day, when first the House leadership group and then the entire House Republican membership had made it clear to Gingrich that they would rather shut down the government than capitulate to the White House, how could the speaker return only twelve hours later with an idea like this? The memo was quickly slipped to DeLay, who reacted as his aides expected. He marched up to Armey's office.

"We can't do this," DeLay said. "Our members will kill us!" The majority leader agreed.

By the time Gingrich distributed the memo later that morning at a meeting of his kitchen cabinet, known as the Speaker's Advisory Group, or SAG, his top lieutenants had lined up solidly against him. They agreed with his assumptions, they said, but not with his timing. They felt they had been playing too much defense and were, as DeLay put it, "tired of being snookered" by the White House. The Democrats were pounding them in the media by successfully linking legislative tactics with a communications strategy, spending millions of dollars in television ads attacking the Republicans on Medicare and tax cuts for the wealthy. The school lunch debacle back in February looked tame by comparison. DeLay and his boys said it was time to stop "acting like a bunch of chumps" and fight back.

Gingrich was frustrated by the resistance, but soon relented, for the second time in two days backing away from his position not to allow the government to close. He became invigorated as SAG members worked on a revised mission based on the speaker's favorite mode of operation, which early on he had called VSTP—Vision, Strategy, Tactics, Projects. Starting then and for the rest of the struggle over the balanced budget, they decided, they would attempt to define their vision and strategy and follow through each day with tactics and projects. While Gingrich and his colleagues—including Armey, DeLay, Boehner, Kasich, Walker, Senators Paul Coverdell of Georgia and Connie Mack of Florida, and Governor Engler—began writing a vision statement, their communications aides repaired to another room to devise a set of tactics. An easel was brought into the Dinosaur Room and Gingrich and Coverdell alternated as group leaders in a series of long weekend meetings.

After scratching and revising, they arrived at a vision statement which they ripped off the easel and posted on the wall above a bust of Thomas Jefferson. It read:

> The American people want a 7-year balanced budget using honest numbers which saves Medicare, returns power to families and state and local governments, reforms welfare, provides tax relief for families and job creation. We will take the necessary steps to achieve enactment by the end of the first session of the 104th Congress.

If nothing else, it was a process that made them feel better about themselves. "We changed history today," said DeLay as he left the room the first day. "We're not buying any more b.s."

On the other end of Pennsylvania Avenue, President Clinton had convened a meeting that Saturday morning at Blair House with some forty Democratic members of Congress. In contrast to the Republican SAG, the core group here went by the acronym BAG (Bicameral Advisory Group), which was formed to assist the Democratic negotiating team in the budget talks.

The president opened the meeting by indicating that he wanted to become personally engaged in the process. The congressmen talked to him for three hours, expressing a range of disparate views on the budget, then returned to the largely deserted Capitol Hill for more weekend sessions where they began putting together a budget plan all Democrats might agree on. Clinton's aides knew that sooner or later they would have to present a budget that could be scored as balanced by the Congressional Budget Office. They hoped it would be later.

ON Monday morning, December 18, the first workday of the second government shutdown, the Democratic task force met in a hearing room in the Dirksen Senate Office Building to continue work on their consensus budget. The White House contingent included Leon Panetta, George Stephanopoulos, and Clinton pollster Stan Greenberg. The pollster was the first speaker. Greenberg cited his latest surveys showing that Democrats were holding strong in public opinion and that Republicans were bearing most of the blame for the shutdown. No one said it aloud, but some in the room thought it was a bit unseemly to begin the meeting with poll numbers.

Later, back at the White House, Clinton and his aides decided that they did not want to appear as obstructionists and needed to devise a plan to get the Republicans back to the table. It was perhaps not coincidental that the stock market was dropping 101.52 points that day. At a strategy session in the Oval Office, they discussed how they could present Gingrich and Dole with a set of options to lure them back. Deputy chief of staff Erskine Bowles suggested one option would be to agree to present a seven-year budget scored by CBO on the condition that the Republicans dropped their Medicare and Medicaid cuts. Clinton suggested another option: unconditional talks with him in the room. A third option would be to work with a menu of budget plans, including those being developed on Capitol Hill.

Satisfied with the strategy, Clinton placed phone calls to Dole and Gingrich. The call to Dole was short and sweet. They talked about resuming the talks and the possibilities of working out a short-term CR to end the shutdown. Dole liked the idea of getting Clinton in the room, and was ready and willing to join him.

If they could do it alone, Dole suggested, they could work out an agreement in no time.

The call to Gingrich lasted nearly twenty minutes. The president and the speaker are both known as gabbers, so when their aides listen to them work the phone they are accustomed to hearing their boss do most of the talking. This time, after it was over, both Clinton aides and Gingrich aides made the observation that their man could not seem to get a word in edgewise, which probably meant it was an even match.

The conversation began with an exchange of accusations of bad faith. Clinton complained about a series of attacks against him on the House floor the previous week challenging his interest in the negotiations. "In all due respect," responded Gingrich, "we don't think one-point-five million dollars in ads bought Friday morning was in good faith, either."

Clinton said the Republicans were acting irresponsibly by refusing to open the government. Gingrich, who privately agreed that his troops should support a CR, did not say that to the president. "You may not trust us, but frankly our members are not in a very trusting mood, either," he said, adding: "Look, you have to see it from our point of view. We've written a three-thousand-page document. Our members have taken a lot of tough votes. We've hiked all the way to the top of the mountain wearing backpacks and now you're driving three-quarters of the way up in a camper and want equal credit."

As Gingrich went on, Clinton felt compelled to interrupt him once with a gentle jab of humor. "Come on, Newt, lighten up," he said. "You're Man of the Year!"

It was a reference to Gingrich's selection as *Time* magazine's most important figure of 1995.

"Yeah, well, George Bush told me, as long as you don't have two faces on the cover you're doing well," Gingrich responded.

"Hey," said Clinton, "they made me an X-ray"—a reference to an April 1992 cover of *Time* featuring a photographic negative of Clinton's face with the headline: "Why Voters Don't Trust Clinton."

It was classic Clinton. His easygoing conversational style would soften Gingrich time and again. Soon the speaker had agreed to visit the White House the next day with Dole to begin face-to-face meetings with the president. The principals, it was agreed, should be able to answer the big questions. Kasich and Domenici and Panetta would now be called advisers. Two long sessions, Gingrich said, should be enough to determine whether there was a deal or a stalemate.

LATE that afternoon, in Room HC-4 in the basement of the Capitol, Boehner called an emergency meeting of the Thursday Group. Paul Coverdell, his coalition counterpart from the Senate, was at Boehner's side. They had placed two big posters on a wall, one with the vision statement written over the weekend, the second with a list of strategies.

"Everything has changed," Coverdell told the group. "We need a more activist approach. We now have to micromanage the battle by the day and week. We're fighting against a presidential campaign, so we'll have to put up one of our own."

Coverdell said that two years ago he met with Dick Morris, the Machiavellian political operator who then was a consultant to Republicans and was now advising Clinton. He went back and found the notes from that meeting, and saw a quote from Morris that jumped off the page: "He who defines first, defines last."

Boehner described the telephone conversation that day between Gingrich and Clinton. "Some of you may get calls for money" to pay for Republican National Committee response ads to the Democrats, he said. "We want to change the daily tracking numbers for Clinton. We're not going to get him to move until he feels the heat." The coalitions needed to get their grass-roots fax networks into high gear, he went on.

That night in the Senate majority leader's office, Dole, Gingrich, Kasich, Domenici, and their staffs met to go over what Dole and Gingrich would do at the White House the next day. It was agreed that their mission was a simple one: They were supposed to demand that Clinton put a CBO-scored balanced budget plan on the table. That was it. No discussion of other options. If Clinton balked, they were going to leave. They would not get sucked in. They would force Clinton to show his hand.

There was another huddle in Dole's office Tuesday morning before the drive to the White House. Armey and DeLay were there, along with Kasich to bolster Gingrich's resolve. Nail them down. Don't negotiate about the negotiations, they told him. He would try not to, Gingrich said, but acknowledged that something seemed to happen to him whenever he got in a room with Clinton.

THE White House session lasted two hours. The more it dragged on, the more worried Republicans outside the Oval Office became. The joke over in DeLay's shop was that it was four to one in that room—Clinton, Gore, Panetta, and Dole versus Newt. But the joke made them nervous. What was going on in there? It does not take two hours to present a simple demand.

In fact, everything was proceeding according to plan—the White House plan, that is. In a pre-meeting strategy session, Clinton and his aides had agreed that they would do everything possible to delay presenting a new White House balanced budget proposal. As soon as they did that, it would become the baseline for all future negotiations. Clinton wanted more room to maneuver. When Dole and Gingrich arrived, he presented all the options and argued that it would be easier to get the negotiations started if the White House did not have to put down a new CBO-scored plan of its own. "If we put one down, you guys are just going to attack it," he said.

Rather than sticking to their demand, and refusing to negotiate about the negotiations, Gingrich and Dole accepted Clinton's argument. They agreed to negotiate from a menu of proposals that could be scored as balanced by the CBO, including the Republican plan and several measures floating on Capitol Hill drafted by conservative Democrats and bipartisan coalitions. The fact that Clinton committed himself to being personally involved encouraged the Republican leaders. "That's worth something," Gingrich thought to himself.

Dan Meyer made a note that the White House seemed willing to go to great lengths to avoid putting a plan on the table. He tried to get his boss to slow down, but to no avail. Meyer became even more concerned near the end of the meeting when Vice President Gore summarized the proceedings. In his summary, as he was discussing the menu of plans that would be used in the negotiations, he included the old White House plan. It happened quickly, and Meyer did not think Gore was trying to be manipulative, but it set off alarm bells with Gingrich's aide because the White House plan did not achieve a CBO-scored balanced budget in seven years. He did not think Gingrich and Dole had agreed to that.

As the meeting was breaking up, Meyer whispered to Panetta, "This could be a problem."

Panetta nodded and said, "Let me take a look tomorrow."

Clinton closed the meeting by asking for an unconditional continuing resolution to reopen the government through the end of the year while the negotiations were taking place. That was too much, Gingrich said, and if he tried to push it on his members, "you'll be dealing with Speaker Armey"—not a pleasing thought for Clinton and his aides, who regarded Armey as the most obstinate and prickly member of the rival team. Gingrich agreed to go back and ask the House for a short-term resolution to keep the government running through the end of the week. It was agreed that the principals would get together again the next day after the advisers met to set the ground rules.

Kasich and Domenici, who did not like being reduced to the status of advisers, were waiting outside the room. They were stunned to hear the results of the summit. For weeks they had refused to bargain with Panetta until he put a CBO-scored budget on the table. They had urged Dole and Gingrich to demand one. Instead, Kasich thought, they "screwed up the whole deal" by not forcing Clinton's hand. "Geez, we could have done what you did a long time ago," he said.

On the ride back to the Capitol in Dole's car, Meyer and Sheila Burke, who was there with Dole, raised their concerns about Gore's wrap-up of the meeting in which he included the White House plan in the talks. Gingrich and Dole seemed optimistic. They thought the talks were back on track, that Clinton was ready to deal, and they went up to the Senate Press Gallery to tell the world about their accomplishments. Gingrich announced what he thought were the key points of movement: The president would be personally engaged; only plans that were CBO-scored ahead of time could be on the table; and they would get a deal before the end of the year.

The White House team watched Gingrich on C-SPAN. Gore stiffened when he heard the speaker declare that the White House plan, which was not CBO-scored, would not be part of the discussions. "We can't let that stand," he said. "We never agreed to that!" He marched down to the White House press briefing room and offered a response. He said that the White House plan would be on the table, that it did not have to be scored by CBO until after the negotiations were settled, and that there was no guarantee that a deal could be reached before the end of the year.

Meyer, who had anticipated the misunderstanding, received word from his office that Gore was challenging Gingrich. Using his cellular phone, he placed a call to Pat Griffin, the White House congressional lobbyist. Upon hanging up, Meyer and Griffin reported their conversation differently. Griffin said Meyer essentially conceded that Gingrich had gone too far and that Gore had to say something. Meyer reported that he got the impression from Griffin that the White House did not want to make it explicit that their plan wasn't on the table. They would find that embarrassing, he said.

FROM the press gallery, Gingrich took the underground tunnels of the Capitol over to the cavernous Caucus Room at 345 Cannon House Office Building where his Republican following awaited him again. He sounded an optimistic note at first as he recounted his dealings with Clinton, but when he started to mention the need for what he described as a "short-leash" continuing resolution, the crowd grew surly.

"What in the world do you want to give them a CR for?" asked Greg Ganske, a moderate freshman from Iowa.

One by one, members took the floor to denounce the agreement. Opening the government would just give the White House more slack, they argued. The House Republicans were already getting blamed for everything, so what more was there to lose? The only way to get a balanced budget now was to keep the government closed and make it a crisis. "You've got to pound those guys!" shouted one moderate congressman. "Don't give them an inch!"

"Have you ever trained a dog?" Gingrich said, trying to explain his approach. "You need to use both sugar and a stick."

At which point freshman Tom Coburn of Oklahoma stood up and shouted, "Well, this dog's got distemper!"

Gingrich's leadership team looked on in dismay. They had known all along what the public could not see: That Gingrich, for all his tough talk, was essentially a softie. Nobody pictured Newt melting like an ice-cream cone, thought Boehner, but that's what he would do. That's what he did at the White House. The guy just did not like to say no. He loved to sit in the White House. He loved to contemplate his role in history. He even loved to talk to Bill Clinton. But now he seemed on the verge of losing his rank-and-file, and his lieutenants were troubled by the thought. None of them felt they could or should openly challenge Gingrich for control. But if he lost his troops, the result would be only chaos.

Gingrich, for his part, was aware of the squeeze he was in. He wanted to keep the negotiations going, believing deeply that the only way to sustain the momentum of the revolution was to strike a deal before the end of the year. He wanted to maintain his partnership with Dole, who considered the House Republicans reckless. But he knew that strategically he was still too far out in front of his membership. He could sense things falling apart again.

After the Republican conference, Panetta and Griffin met with the budget chairmen, Domenici and Kasich, and GOP leadership aides in a small unmarked room known as "Domenici's Hideaway" in the lower recesses of the Capitol. The room was decorated in a western motif and offered a brilliant nighttime view down the Mall of the sparkling Christmas tree and Washington Monument. Kasich and Domenici were not in a celebratory mood. They had been assigned to work with Panetta to set up the ground rules for the next day's session of the principals, and were clearly "yanked off," as one leadership aide later put it, frustrated by what had transpired at the White House that day.

When it was over and Panetta and the Republican staffers had left, Kasich and Domenici sat alone and drank some of Domenici's wine. They were quite a pair, the budget chairs, Domenici as placid and precise as Kasich was exuberant and freewheeling. Domenici told Kasich stories about the old days, back in 1981, when the Reagan Revolution started to slip away. The two of them made a vow that they would stick together and try to get back to the negotiating table with the principals. They were, after all, the only ones who really knew this stuff.

The plans for the next day made down at Domenici's office were being undone in any case upstairs in the Dinosaur Room, where Gingrich was holding yet another meeting with his advisory group. DeLay, eager to hold off the latest Gingrich push for a short-leash CR, had brought in a videotape of Gore's speech and kept insisting that the speaker and the others watch it. Gingrich refused at first, but finally relented.

The tape did not improve his mood. DeLay watched with satisfaction as Gingrich bit on his lower lip and turned red with anger. There were times during the showing of the Gore tape when the room rocked with derisive laughter, but the underlying mood was one of crisis and outrage. It reminded the House Republicans of that day a month earlier when the Democrats had signed a deal promising to present a CBO-scored balanced budget in exchange for a resolution to reopen the government. The November 19 pact was taking on mythical resonance. It was the Alamo of the Republican Revolution. "Remember November!" became the battle cry.

TWELVE

"You're Just Being the Beaver!"

LARGE POLITICAL AND historical forces were at work in the great balanced budget fight, but in the middle of it all, shaping events and being shaped by them, were three formidable politicians: One who was president; one who wanted to be president; and one who sometimes acted as though he were president. The personalities and characters of Bill Clinton, Bob Dole, and Newt Gingrich often seemed as pivotal in the budget end game as the arguments over Medicare, tax cuts, and spending for welfare, education, and the environment. That was never more true than during the period that began on Wednesday morning, December 20, the fifth day of the second government shutdown.

The television set in House Minority Leader Dick Gephardt's office was tuned to C-SPAN that morning when Leon Panetta and several aides arrived for their morning round of meetings at the Capitol. The first scene they witnessed on the screen was a stunner, particularly in contrast with newspaper headlines that morning trumpeting progress in the budget talks and the likelihood that the federal government would reopen after a five-day shutdown. There, live on television, was Tom DeLay, standing in the well of the House floor, declaring that there would be no move by the House Republicans to reopen the government.

This was good news and bad news for the White House team.

The bad news was that if DeLay was correct, Gingrich had lost another internal battle and the short-leash continuing resolution that had been agreed upon at the White House the day before was now dead. The good news was that this would make it easy for Democrats to spend the day blaming the shutdown on the Republicans. President Clinton's instincts were to show the White House always trying to keep the balanced budget talks going and to reopen the government. He wanted always to give the appearance of forward movement. It was largely a matter, as one White House aide said, of "staying one step ahead of the blame."

Gingrich had indeed already lost that morning. His Speaker's Advisory Group had held another rollicking meeting in the Dinosaur Room and voted 12 to 0 not to do a short-term continuing resolution. Once that had been decided, Gingrich said it was important for the House Republicans to make a unified declaration of their unhappiness with the White House. Conference Chairman Boehner persuaded Congressman Scott Klug of Wisconsin to present a resolution stating that the House would not approve a continuing resolution until the White House presented a CBO-scored balanced budget.

Accepting the stubbornness of his troops was easier for Gingrich than explaining it again to Bob Dole and Leon Panetta. This entire negotiating process had made him increasingly envious of the Senate and White House. Dole and Clinton could act virtually autonomously. Dole didn't seem to care much what his leadership thought. He would just say and do what he wanted. Clinton had the same freedom. But Gingrich, for all his preoccupation with corporate management theory, was encumbered by the democratic notions of the people's House. He was trying to find ways to have the same freedom of movement as Dole and Clinton, but it was not easy. His advisory group made that point explicit this morning—and now he had to pass the word along.

The budget advisers, Kasich and Domenici, were with Panetta down in Domenici's Hideaway, and Gingrich and Dole were supposed to see Panetta soon to go over the day's schedule. Gingrich realized now that the meeting would be fruitless. He would have to tell Panetta himself. But first he walked over to Dole's office to break the news.

"I know you don't agree with this strategy and I'm willing to meet with Panetta on my own," Gingrich said, after explaining that the House had again rejected the notion of a continuing resolution.

"Well, don't they want a balanced budget?" asked Dole, clearly irritated at the House Republicans.

"Yeah, they want a balanced budget, but they don't think they can get one trusting this guy," said Gingrich. "I'm willing to meet with Panetta alone if that's what you want me to do."

"Yeah," said Dole. "Why don't you meet with Panetta."

Before Gingrich left, he and Dole engaged in a conversation about the man with whom they were dealing. They tried to explain Bill Clinton, and to read his mind.

"You know that movie *National Lampoon's Christmas Vacation,* when the Chevy Chase character is at the store with his cousin?" Gingrich began.

Dole displayed a surprising command of pop culture. At an earlier meeting, when Kasich had told him that he was negotiating with some conservative Democrats who went by the political nickname of "Blue Dogs," Dole had said, "We don't have any Blue Dogs in the Senate. We have some hot dogs. And we've got Snoop Doggy Dogg." This time he understood immediately what movie Gingrich was talking about. "Yeah," Dole said, "Cousin Willie."

Clinton, Gingrich said, reminded him of that character.

"That scene where Chevy Chase says to him, 'We're really worried about your kids and we want to help them get gifts.' And the cousin says, 'Oh, no, you shouldn't.' And Chevy Chase says, 'Oh, no we really want to.' And the guy goes, 'No, that would be like taking welfare.' And he says, 'Oh, no we really want to help you.'

And the cousin says, 'Well, I happen to have a list in my pocket.' Then he says, as Chase is looking at the list, 'By the way, why don't you buy yourself something?' "

Clinton could play that role with a straight face, Gingrich said. "He knows how to maneuver you into a position that on a normal day you'd realize was utterly irrational."

Dole had been doing his own thinking about Clinton. He was always looking for reasons why Clinton would want to make the budget deal. For weeks he had been arguing that Clinton would come to the table because he had relied so heavily on Dole to support his position on Bosnia. Now he had a new theory.

"The president wants a deal, you know why?" Dole said. "Whitewater. I've been thinking about this. He's got to find something to get that off the front pages."

Gingrich was uncertain about that reasoning. Had anyone at the White House been eavesdropping on the conversation, they would have scratched their heads. If anything, Whitewater was driving Clinton away from a deal. Political adviser James Carville, who opposed a budget deal, would often say to the president, "Look, you're dealing with people who are screwing you every day on Whitewater. Why are you giving them so much?"

GINGRICH returned to his office and sent an aide down to Domenici's Hideaway to get Panetta, who walked up to the Dinosaur Room accompanied by Pat Griffin.

"Trouble in River City, eh?" Panetta said, looking concerned as he entered.

"I realize you're going to be upset with this turn of events. We can't do a CR," Gingrich said. "I fully expect this will blow things up for a day or two. I understand. Our people are just not willing to move forward."

The meeting turned into a confessional of sorts during which both sides sought to explain themselves, the internal dynamics they faced, and their perceptions from across the table.

"Our guys figure they've probably taken your best hits on Medicare and they don't have much more to lose," Gingrich said. "They're staking their political careers on getting a balanced budget. Frankly, they're not going to budge in any way that would compromise that goal. You hit us with thirty million dollars in advertising, but frankly when we came back and won California [the special congressional election won December 12 by Republican Tom Campbell], that made them think that a lot of this stuff isn't going to stick at election time."

Pat Griffin used the same distancing technique, explaining the mind-set of other Democrats and how that affected the White House. "The president wants to rise above this and get a deal," he said. "But we have a situation where a lot of our guys are polling around the clock—and this is working for them. They blame the shutdown on you. Make you look like extremists. It's getting very difficult to move them because they think politics is on the side of doing nothing."

Panetta sighed. "Man, this is tough," he said. "We've never been in a situation like this. There's a problem with chemistry. Your guys are locking up and our guys are locking up. Until we change the chemistry it's going to be hard to move things. There's some concern that if at some point we do get a deal, a compromise, are you going to be able to deliver the votes?"

"When we do have a deal, if it's with an authentic balanced budget, we'll be able to deliver the votes," said Gingrich.

Gingrich returned to the topic he had explored earlier with Dole—the effect Bill Clinton had on him.

"I've got a problem. I get in those meetings and as a person I like the president," Gingrich said. "I melt when I'm around him. After I get out, I need two hours to detoxify. My people are nervous about me going in there because of the way I deal with this."

Panetta and Griffin laughed.

"We've got the same problem on the other side," Panetta said. "People are nervous about Clinton going in and talking too much."

After Panetta and Griffin left, Gingrich muttered, "This is draining stuff. I like to give speeches. It's more fun."

* * *

TWICE that day, President Clinton had called Bob Dole, first to commiserate on the turn of events in the House. Was there any way Dole could move something in the Senate that could pick up House votes? Clinton asked. Then something extraordinary happened, made possible only by the peculiar turn of events that had brought Clinton and Dole somehow, temporarily, together. The president began thinking like a campaign manager for the man who wanted to replace him in the White House in 1996. "Isn't there some way you can get House members who've endorsed you to help you out on this?" Clinton asked.

The second call was a heads-up from Clinton that he was about to head down to the White House press briefing room to lambaste the House for refusing to reopen the government. Dole offered a halfhearted argument against the move, but privately felt much the same way himself. They agreed that if left alone, they could reopen the government and balance the budget in no time. After hanging up, Clinton turned to his aides, smiled, and said, "My new best friend—Bob Dole!"

The president then left for the briefing room and told reporters that "the most extreme members of the House" had scuttled the negotiations. The buzz around town, encouraged by Clinton and his staff, was that radicals in the House freshman class had taken over the chamber and Gingrich had lost control. If only it were that simple, Gingrich and his aides thought.

AT eight o'clock the next morning, December 21, Panetta traveled up to the Capitol to have breakfast with his familiar foes, Domenici and Kasich. The mission for the three advisers was to get the talks started again. Both sides agreed that they would only look worse if they refused to meet at a time when the government was still partially closed. Panetta proposed that the advisers work on second-tier budget issues that day and that the principals reconvene in the Oval Office the next day, then take four days off for Christmas and come back and negotiate some more. In the meantime, he said, Congress should put a continuing resolution in place through January 3.

"Look, there's no way you're going to get a CR!" said Kasich, who had taken an increasingly hard line since Tuesday, when he was left distraught by the way Gingrich and Dole had seemed to fold at the White House. "Just forget it. We spent thirty days going nowhere while we had a CR."

"John, I want to be candid with you," said Panetta. "You're never going to get what you want using the kind of tactics you're using right now."

Domenici changed the subject. He had been thinking about how clever the Democrats seemed. He decided to praise Panetta while jabbing him at the same time.

"You guys have been brilliant the way you did this using the OMB budget," Domenici said. "You're able to go around the country talking about how you have a balanced budget, too. But you never had to meet the test that we met. The country doesn't know this. They can't tell the difference between OMB and CBO. I commend you on your political strategy, because it was brilliant."

Then he paused, focused more intensely on Panetta, and said, "I just have to ask you: Weren't you a little embarrassed with the offer that you brought in on the fifteenth of December that did absolutely nothing?"

There was a moment of silence before Panetta responded. "Not as a negotiator, I wasn't embarrassed," he said.

The three men spent most of the day together, surrounded by aides, as they went over balanced budget issues on which both sides could agree—mostly parts that were identical or nearly so in the opposing plans. Kasich was in a foul mood. A few weeks earlier, at a Republican caucus, he had vowed to keep cool throughout the negotiations and pretend he was "Bond—James Bond." So much for that bit of miscasting. Panetta and Griffin wanted to end the meeting with an agreement that both sides would leave the room and issue positive statements to the press. Kasich wanted none of it. "We didn't do anything today," he said. "I'm not going to go out there and say everything's great when we're not going anywhere!" Griffin kept pushing, and Kasich finally relented.

"If you want to say the talks were constructive, go ahead," he said.

SPEAKER Gingrich made a rare appearance that day at the Thursday Group of Boehner and his lobbyists. The speaker walked in, unannounced, five minutes into the session, and quickly took over. "How much would all of you pay for a budget agreement?" he asked.

The question was met with silence. No one was quite sure what he meant.

"How much of the tax cut would the business community be willing to give up to get a budget deal?"

The typical lobbyist might wait his entire career before receiving such a blunt question. Everyone knew that sooner or later the Republicans would come down on their tax cuts to make a deal. Now, it seemed, Gingrich was finally making the move.

"Whatever you do with a tax cut, take care of the priorities of the constituencies that made you a majority," said Dirk Van Dongen of the National Association of Wholesaler-Distributors. "Something for small business. Cap gains. And families."

"I don't think you should be so much concerned with how much taxes are cut but whose," said Mark Isakowitz, a lobbyist for the National Federation of Independent Business. "From the small business perspective," he said, "if you deliver on estate tax relief and increase the equipment expense limit, we'll know we got something."

"What if we give you guys estate taxes but sunset it in 1998?" Gingrich asked. "That's an election year. No one is going to let your tax cut expire. But it helps us get a deal now. Would you go along?"

Yes, Isakowitz said, but only if it was fair across the board and other groups had their tax cuts sunset as well.

Gingrich also told the group of a conversation he had with George Shultz, the former labor secretary and secretary of state in previous Republican administrations. They had first talked on

Air Force One during the plane ride to Jerusalem for Israeli Prime
Minister Yitzhak Rabin's funeral, then Shultz had sent Gingrich
a paper he had written on the lessons he had learned negotiating as
Reagan's secretary of state. Gingrich followed it up with a phone
call. No deal is better than a bad deal, Shultz said, and it is important to place yourself "in a position to handle a no-deal environment." Shultz compared the budget negotiations to his dealings
with the Soviets during the early 1980s. "They always wanted a reward just for coming to the table," Shultz told Gingrich. He made
the analogy to Clinton wanting the reward of a CR for continuing
the negotiations. "You don't give rewards for that."

Along with the business world, there was another key element of
the conservative movement that Gingrich and his leadership team
had to check with as they moved toward a possible compromise:
the Christian right. Kasich, a born-again Christian, served as the
intermediary in talks with Pat Robertson and Ralph Reed of the
Christian Coalition. The religious right had a special interest in
the $500-per-child tax break for families, which was a plank in a so-
cial contract they had proposed as a follow-up to the Contract with
America. To lessen the budget impact of the tax cut, Kasich wanted
it to be means-tested so that only families earning less than $70,000
a year would qualify. Robertson said that was acceptable with him.
Reed, at a lunch with Kasich, pressed for a higher number.

THE Republican negotiating team met at ten o'clock the next morning—December 22—in Dole's office before driving over to the
White House. Along with Gingrich, Dole, Kasich, and Domenici,
there was a new member of the group: Dick Armey. His Texas
buddy, Tom DeLay, had urged that Armey be added to the
group partly to strengthen Gingrich's resolve. "You need someone
in the room to watch your back," DeLay had told the speaker. There
was more to it than that. The Republican freshmen wanted Armey
in the room because they were losing some faith in Gingrich.
The rest of the leadership team wanted Armey in the room because Gingrich seemed to be getting more remote and testy as he

took on more of the burden himself. Kasich wanted Armey in the room because he considered Gingrich a hapless negotiator. In his metaphor-rich, jocular style, Kasich said sharply of Gingrich: "We keep going to the bazaar and he keeps buying rugs, and he has a station wagon full of them every day and every night he says, 'Honey, I'm not very good at this. But did you see my newest rug?' "

So Armey would be in the room. Tough and dependable. Yet it was Armey who sounded the most conciliatory and optimistic during the meeting at Dole's office. "I'm not out to be the bad cop in this whole thing," he said. "We have to go down there and be positive because one short word will be played by the other side as us blowing up the talks." Gingrich and Dole were also feeling upbeat. Dole had just been recognized by his colleagues as the longest-serving GOP leader in the Senate. Even some Democratic senators congratulated him privately by saying they looked forward to President Dole. Kasich and Domenici were less sanguine. They wondered what could possibly be accomplished until the White House presented what they considered a legitimate offer.

It turned out that the Democrats had no intention of talking offers on this day during the meeting in the Cabinet Room. They had a long agenda that involved having staff members brief them on all the major issues, from each perspective, starting with Medicare and Medicaid. Clinton asked most of the questions, totally engaged as the policy wonk, often drawing his fellow traveler Gingrich into arcane points of inquiry. Kasich seemed the least intimidated by the president. Once, when Clinton said he agreed with "Mr. Kasich" on a point, the irrepressible Ohioan turned to Panetta and whispered, "See, Leon, you dumb shit?"

After a few hours, Clinton, Vice President Gore, and Panetta took Dole, Gingrich, and Armey into the Oval Office to discuss how to proceed from there. Panetta said the staffs should meet the following Wednesday, the 27th, followed by the advisers on Thursday, and the principals on Friday. Armey and Gingrich said they were ready to meet over the weekend if need be, but the Democrats said they needed the time off for personal reasons.

When they adjourned, Panetta came into the Roosevelt Room

where Republican staff members had been waiting and announced the schedule. The aides breathed a sigh of relief about getting four days off, then remembered that the government was still shut down. Paranoid thoughts creeped in. How do we do this with a shutdown? Are we being set up? But Gingrich was happy on the ride home. He liked the way the meeting was set up, with the president seated in the middle and Gingrich right next to him on one side and Dole on the other, not across the table. It was not much, but he was looking for even small signs of hope.

He felt the year slipping away.

TEN days later, Gingrich ran smack up against his worst fear. It had been nagging at him for a while, but he kept shoving the thought aside. Now he faced it head-on, and the realization sent him into a depression. It hit him as he was riding back to the Capitol from the White House on the evening of Tuesday, January 2, 1996. He had screwed up. Everything he had done was based on the wrong premises, the wrong reading of his adversary. He had grievously miscalculated his opposition and strategically botched the most important political battle of his speakership.

He had just spent several hours in the Oval Office listening to President Clinton and the White House negotiating team explain their latest balanced budget proposal. Beforehand, he had thought that a breakthrough might be imminent. After endless policy discussions over the previous ten days, the White House had indicated that it was ready to talk about a real deal. Finally there might be movement toward a compromise and with it an end to the crippling and unpopular government shutdown, which was entering its third week.

But was there in fact anything new in what Clinton and the Democrats, using an easel and arrows and encouraging words, had presented on that evening of January 2? When he was in the Oval Office, Gingrich thought so, as did his negotiating partners, Armey and Bob Dole. Clinton could do that to them, the speaker thought. His body language, his speech patterns, the way he would say he liked your tie, his ability to convince people of a sense of joint effort and joint understanding, made the president "one of the most compelling developers of mood" that Gingrich had ever encountered.

Yet with every passing minute that he was out of the Oval Office, away from Clinton, Gingrich grew more dubious. When he first saw his aides in the Roosevelt Room afterwards and they asked him to rank the evening's negotiations on a scale of one to ten, with one meaning no deal and ten meaning a deal, he had given them a four. On the car ride back to the Capitol, he was feeling even less optimistic. Piece by piece, he began reconstructing that night's talks to examine the reasons for his growing unease. After all this time, Clinton still would not make significant moves on Medicare and Medicaid, the entitlement programs that were at the center of the Republican budget-balancing effort. The Democrats were invoking "absolute moral necessity" as a reason for their intransigence, Gingrich told his staff. His own team, he said, was put at the disadvantage of searching for middle ground.

When he got back to his office on the second floor of the Capitol, Gingrich called his wife, Marianne, who had been a valuable sounding board during the negotiations. "You know, this doesn't feel right, but let me tell you where we're at," he said. The more he talked to his wife, the more he realized that for all the atmospherics of compromise and movement that night, "there had eloquently been no movement." The outer boundaries of where Clinton and his team would go now seemed clear to Gingrich, and the realization stunned him. All fall and winter, he had believed that Clinton in the end would move to the center to make a deal. He thought he understood Clinton. Trent Lott, Gingrich's old friend, the Senate majority whip who was close to Clinton's consultant, Dick Morris, kept telling the speaker that a deal was inevitable.

Small doubts had been seeping into Gingrich's mind since December 15, when the Clinton team had failed to put a serious balanced budget proposal on the table after the Republicans thought they had been promised one. Now those doubts had hardened into certainty. He had utterly misread the entire budget end game.

The deal was not going to happen. Clinton, he concluded, had a "George Bush problem." The president had drawn such a hard line on Medicare and Medicaid that to move away from it would make him look as weak as Bush looked in 1990 when he backed away from his "No New Taxes" pledge. For the first time, Gingrich said later, "the realization hit me that it was very likely going to prove to be impossible to get to an agreement." The thought made him weary and depressed.

How could he have been so naive? Gingrich wondered. Why had he kept believing that Clinton was about to compromise? Marianne Gingrich said it reminded her of an episode from the old television sitcom *Leave It to Beaver*. The Beaver was walking home with a pocketful of money he had earned and ran into a hobo, who managed to talk him out of it by relating a sob story about his life. Beaver's older brother laughed when he heard what happened and asked, "How could you do that, Beaver? You knew the story wasn't true." And Beaver said, "Yeah, but it was such a good story and I felt so good doing it."

"Newt," said Marianne Gingrich to the Speaker of the House. "You're just being the Beaver!"

That night of January 2 marked another turning point in the balanced budget end game and the beginning of one of the most exhausting and politically complicated weeks of Gingrich's time running the House. After putting a year's worth of effort into a balanced budget endeavor that he expected to be the defining legislative accomplishment of his conservative revolution, he had to deal with a sobering reality: There might not be an ending to the end game. He faced the difficult task of convincing his troops that the battleground had shifted and they had to shift with it. The confrontational shutdown policy, which he had never thought wise, would be impossible to sustain for the long term. He felt a need to "outline a strategy for success" that allowed the Republican House to "feel that it had not betrayed its beliefs."

After a sleepless night, Gingrich met at seven-thirty the next morning, Wednesday, January 3, with a group of assistants and close allies. Former Reagan aide Ken Duberstein was there, along with Don Fierce from the Republican National Committee; Meyer, Gingrich's chief of staff; policy aide Arne Christenson; Governor John Engler; Dick Armey; longtime political adviser Joe Gaylord; and Chuck Boyd, a former Air Force officer who had been a prisoner of war in Vietnam for seven years.

Everything the House had tried from November to then had led nowhere, Gingrich said. "We have to rethink this. We've reached a dead end." He had thought that Clinton would move to the center, but he had been wrong. "They will not agree to anything we would regard as a good deal," he said. "What they are going to offer us is a repetitive series of bad deals, which they will then mischaracterize. We had better design a strategy which both takes into account that they are trapped in the left and that they will mischaracterize what is happening."

The shutdown strategy had obviously failed, argued Meyer. Rather than forcing the White House to compromise, the shutdown was only obscuring the larger Republican campaign for a balanced budget. The split between the House and Senate was widening. The day before, Dole had gone to the Senate floor, declared that "Enough is enough," and dispatched a resolution through his chamber to try to end the shutdown. He had invited Gingrich over to his office and warned him about it beforehand, and the speaker had said he understood. "Well, we'll have to manage the House, and I would not do it at this point, but you're the leader of the Senate and you have to do what you honestly believe in your gut is right," Gingrich had said to Dole. "I'll manage the consequences." But now the first consequences were in the morning newspapers, with headlines screaming about Dole's action and the animosity it had stirred in Gingrich's House.

"Look at this one!" said Fierce, throwing a paper on the table.

"How about this one!" said Duberstein, tossing up another.

Soon five newspapers were there, each headline more troubling than the last.

Gingrich remained protective of Dole. They had to dampen the fires in the House, he said.

"This old soldier knows that one of the most important things is to have unit integrity," said Boyd. "We can't lose that." Boyd sometimes wondered why Gingrich put up with as much as he did.

As soon as possible, Gingrich said, they had to devise a way at least to pay the federal workers who had been suffering since the second shutdown began back on December 15. Since Christmas he had imagined one bad scenario after another. "The next thing that's going to happen," he confided to his staff, "is that some federal worker somewhere in the U.S. is going to commit suicide for some reason and they're going to blame it on the shutdown."

In the middle range, said Duberstein, they should bear in mind that Clinton would face some tough moments in late January and early February. The state of the union address was coming, he noted, and Clinton would want to appear before Congress that night on a positive note. And soon after that, the Clinton administration would have to put out a whole new budget for the next year. They would be forced, finally, Duberstein said, to put down some detailed numbers on how they would cut programs to balance the budget. Without a budget deal, they would have no bipartisan cover for that. Those two factors might still push Clinton toward a late deal.

Armey wondered whether it was worth returning to the White House for more talks. He used a story from his own life to explain his concern. "We keep going back up to the White House and have these wonderful talks and at the end of a long hard day there is nothing concrete. How many times are we willing to go back for that?" Armey said. "Look, guys, I've got some tolerance for that kind of treatment. My wife canceled our wedding three times and I loved her enough to hang around for a fourth time. But there ain't many people I'd be willing to go back to again. They have all the power now because we're the pursuer and they're the pursued."

If nothing else, Armey added a touch of levity to an otherwise somber meeting. "She made a mistake the fourth time," Fierce grumbled about Armey's wife.

The speaker was not in a joking mood. "This is the worst I've felt since Bush was defeated," he said. He confided that he was a dreamer and one of his dreams was being shattered. He had to recover his resolve. Two weeks earlier he had written a memo outlining the dilemma and suggesting that the House reopen the government. He had been overridden that time, but he did not intend for that to happen again.

GINGRICH is a creature of habit, a man of lists, aphorisms, historical allusions, and simple management theories. One of his favorite sayings is that his job as speaker is to listen, learn, help, and lead. From the morning of Wednesday, January 3, through Thursday night, January 4, he mostly listened. He held four leadership meetings and two conferences during that period, spending twenty-two hours in meetings with members of the House. He knew where he wanted to take them: He wanted to end the week with a bill paying the federal workers and possibly reopening the government. But he knew he could not move the House until it was ready to move.

He began his first leadership meeting on Wednesday by saying that the prospects for a deal seemed bleak and then acknowledging his own shortcomings. "Frankly, I thought we'd have this resolved and worked out by now," he said. He had operated on the mistaken theory, he said, that Clinton would collapse and they would have a deal. He was a bad negotiator. What should they do next? What's the condition of the troops?

The question went around the table. Reports came back that some members were getting antsy. Somewhere between twenty-five and forty-five Republicans were ready to break ranks or at least grousing about the pounding they were taking for closing down the government. There was a possibility that the leadership could lose control of the House. Armey said he was disappointed to hear that. Kasich said he'd met with his members that morning and encountered "no buckling."

Gingrich broached the subject of an interim spending bill to reopen the government and another measure to pay federal workers. They were in for a long haul, he said, and he could see that people were getting tired. "Fatigue makes cowards of us all," he said, quoting the late football coach Vince Lombardi. "We've got to find

a way to get our members home. We can't sustain this and keep
everybody together. But we can't do it with this federal worker
issue up in the air."

Bill Archer of the Ways and Means said the shutdown strategy
had backfired and they had to extract themselves from it. But the
very mention of reopening the government enraged other people
in the room. Most of their anger was directed against Dole.

"The Senate is the enemy!" one sophomore thundered.

"Screw the Senate. It's time for all-out war," said DeLay.

Boehner said several House members who had endorsed Dole
were talking about disendorsing him, an idea Boehner was trying
to squash. Armey came to Dole's defense. "He's been with us all
the way in the meeting with the president. Bob Dole is as tough as
any of us!" Armey said.

The leadership discussions were interrupted late in the afternoon
by a negotiating trip to the White House. There was no movement
in the two-plus hours of talks. Vice President Gore told Gingrich,
Dole, and Armey that opposing capital gains cuts was a theologi-
cal issue for the Democrats. On the ride back to the Capitol, Dole
muttered, "Al Gore's driving me nuts."

Clinton left the negotiating session in a happier mood. He had
pushed his staff all day to let him go on television again and blast
the House Republicans as extremists for keeping the government
shut down. The opposition still seemed to be in disarray. The
Democrats were staying one step ahead of the blame.

BY the next morning, Thursday, January 4, Gingrich had the out-
lines of his plan to move the House out of its shutdown policy and pay the federal workers through March 15, a date that
would satisfy Dole because it would clear him of any government headaches while he was campaigning for president in Iowa
and New Hampshire. Leadership opposition was also dissolving.
The whip's office was picking up more signals of members breaking ranks, a fact that was turning Tom DeLay into less of a
hard-liner. He was not ready to lead a revolt against Gingrich in

any case, and the speaker seemed utterly determined this time to prevail.

As the leadership team gathered in their second-floor meeting room, Bill Paxon suggested that the group should do something to let the reporters standing outside the closed doors know that they were unified. "We've got to show them we're together," Paxon said. "Let's let out a cheer." The room reverberated with yips and roars. A few minutes later, Paxon said, "Okay, let's cheer again," and again a roar went up. Gingrich knew he was halfway home.

AT the White House that day, Panetta had invited the two budget chairmen in for lunch. He wanted to give them another version of the pitch that had been delivered to Gingrich, Dole, and Armey on Tuesday. Kasich and Domenici were the ones who knew the numbers, after all, and any deal ultimately would have to go through them, even if they had been reduced to the status of advisers. Tortilla soup was served immediately, and Panetta started eating. "Well, Leon," said Kasich, "are we eating first because you know we won't have an appetite later?" Panetta took three more spoonfuls, then got up and went to the easel.

There were no numbers on the board, just categories and arrows. The first category was a seven-year balanced budget scored by the Congressional Budget Office. The arrow pointed to the Republican side. "CBO. Seven years. That's worth a couple hundred billion dollars each," Panetta said, meaning that by acceding to the Republican request that any budget reach balance in seven years as scored by the conservative estimates of the CBO, the Democrats in effect were giving up that much money right at the start of the negotiations.

"In other words, we owe you big time, huh, Leon?" said Kasich.

"You got it," said Panetta.

The next category was Medicare, with an arrow pointing toward the Democrats.

"We've got to have a win there," said Panetta. "That has to be our win."

Kasich thought it was like some old hackers going over their golf scores deciding who won each hole. Panetta was making the argument that the Republicans should concentrate on the holes they won and brag about them. "Ultimately," he said, "you guys have to sell this."

The budget chairmen returned to Capitol Hill feeling much like Gingrich had two nights earlier. They could not envision a deal.

THE meetings were back to back to back for Gingrich that Thursday afternoon and night. At 2:00 P.M. he had a session with the seventy-three freshmen, who had been getting most of the publicity as the uncontrollable radical faction in his House, a reputation they only partly deserved. There were some rumblings when Gingrich presented his state-of-the-negotiations rap and his plans for easing the House out of its confrontational shutdown position. But it was largely a positive meeting. Sonny Bono got up at one point and declared, "This strategy is brilliant!" which led some in the room to wonder if it should be reassessed.

George Nethercutt of Washington State suggested that if Gingrich wanted to reopen the government with an interim spending bill, he should place the burden of keeping the government closed back on the White House at the same time. One way to do that, Nethercutt said, was to make the resolution reopening the government contingent on the White House presenting a seven-year balanced budget proposal scored by the CBO. Gingrich liked the idea.

In a meeting with the group of moderates known as the Lunch Bunch, Gingrich encountered several members who were dismayed by the shutdown policy and ready to vote with the Democrats to reopen the government. Most of them were heartened by Gingrich's plan. Then came a meeting with the Conservative Action Team, the group that included some of the staunchest members of the freshmen class and their veteran allies. They gave Gingrich the toughest time. Lindsey Graham of South Carolina said he was adamantly opposed to the idea of paying any federal workers who were not on the job.

Graham's statement made sense to Gingrich. He saw that a pay bill had to be linked to a reopening of the government. By listening to Graham and Nethercutt, he had refined his plan. But he had to listen for hours more. The full Republican membership gathered in conference that night for three hours. Several speakers said they could go along with the new plan, but not with extending the bill to keep the government open until March 15. That leash was too long. Gingrich stayed until the last member had his say. "We're not going to make a decision tonight," he said. "Sleep on this and tomorrow we'll get back together to decide where to go."

He then took his leadership team up to Armey's legislative office in the Cannon Building. This was not Newt the softie. This was Newt battling for his life. Anyone who wanted to challenge him would have to fight him for the speakership. He felt his job was on the line. When a few lieutenants tried to raise questions, "he cut their legs off," as one put it. It was clear that his speakership was at risk. Everyone was standing around in a circle when Kasich walked in, with Gingrich in the middle. Pat Roberts, chairman of the Agriculture Committee, slipped into the room and waved his hand in an effort to catch Gingrich's attention. Kasich caught sight of the head Aggie, realized he was in the wrong place at the wrong time, and whispered to him, "Pat, get the fuck out of here."

"I think everyone knew that if they challenged me, I'd call four more meetings," Gingrich said later. "That's the other part of this technique. You have to have the endurance to be the most patient and the most willing to listen, and when you literally burned out everyone else, they will accept leadership out of exhaustion."

THE next morning at 9:30 A.M., Gingrich met with his staff before leaving for a House Republican membership session over in the Cannon Caucus Room. Dole's chief of staff, Sheila Burke, came over for the meeting to hear the final details of Gingrich's plan, which she and her boss would help move simultaneously through the Senate. At long last, Dole would get the House to move on his longstanding plea to reopen the government. Perhaps the House's recalcitrance had helped Dole politically, allowing him to do his own form of triangulation as the voice of reason, the adult, in a shouting match between the House and the White House. But time was slipping away, and he wanted to get on to the primary states and his presidential campaign.

Dan Meyer reminded Gingrich that Denny Hastert, the deputy whip, a bearlike former wrestling coach, had suggested the night before that the entire leadership should line up behind Gingrich physically when he made his pitch to the rank-and-file.

"Yeah," said Gingrich. "We're through listening and learning."

Members were milling around the Caucus Room, joshing, telling stories, when Gingrich marched in.

"All right, everybody sit down!" he shouted.

David Hobson, one of the gentlest souls in the Republican Party, an Ohio congressman known to friends as "Uncle Dave," was hobbling around near the coffee machine. "Hobson! Sit down and shut up!" Gingrich yelled.

"All right," he continued, as the leadership team formed behind him. "We're not taking any vote. I'm not taking any questions. I'm here to tell you what the team's going to do. Now some of you wanted to have a shutdown forever. And that's unsustainable for thirty or forty of our members. So we can't do that.

"Some of you want to do a one-year CR and just give up. And that's unsustainable for a lot of our members. So we're not going to do that, either. This is a team vote and we're going to do this as a team. We're all wearing the same jerseys today. Sometimes you don't agree with the plays that are called. But this is the way we're going."

Gingrich pulled out a piece of paper that described his plan. First, on the House floor, they would vote on a pay bill. Then they would pass an interim spending bill contingent on the White House presenting a balanced budget bill.

"If anybody votes against it, I'm not going to take it out on you," Gingrich said. "I'm not going to punish you." Then he described what sounded like a form of punishment. "But I'm going to keep a list. And if any of you on the list come up to me later and talk about anybody else not being on the team, I don't want to hear about it. If any of you come up and talk about how the team's got to help you out, I don't want to hear about it.

"We're going down now to vote."

The Republicans rose to their feet and applauded, then marched out of the room.

When the roll-call vote on the pay bill was recorded, Gingrich was handed a slip of paper listing the fourteen Republicans who voted against it. He folded the list and slipped it into his wallet.

AT the strategy session at the White House that same day, Friday, January 5, Clinton's aides found it puzzling that the Republicans were placing so much emphasis on forcing them to present a seven-year budget scored by the CBO. They had just such a plan ready, known as the Daschle plan because it was largely crafted by Senate Minority Leader Tom Daschle. "So the Republicans demand a plan, and we put one down—then what do they do?" said one Clinton aide. "We can no longer assume that they have a strategy. We've been there. We were there on health care."

Although Gingrich saw no need to keep meeting with Clinton, he was persuaded by his staff and Dole and Armey to head down to the White House again. Not much of substance was accomplished, but Clinton worked his charm on Armey that night. Of all the Republicans, Clinton seemed to have the hardest time with Armey. Twice, once in public last year and again at a meeting in November, the gruff Texan had insulted the president's wife. Clinton had never seen Armey's sense of humor, or his humanity, until these last few sessions, when Armey came across as a reasonable fellow. At the end of the session, Clinton called Armey over and let him in his circle. "I misjudged you," he said. "I had a sense you were basically a mean person and you're not."

Was the Clinton seduction working its magic again? Armey and Gingrich left the meeting talking about Clinton's body language.

The president was on the edge of his chair, leaning toward them, Armey said. It was as though he wanted to come out of his chair and the others were holding him back. Gore was trying to restrain Clinton. Once when Gore interrupted, trying to slow him down, Clinton said, "Wait a minute, let me finish here." What did it all mean? Maybe the president really was moving toward a deal. Maybe he really wanted one.

Bob Dole was leery of the body language stuff, but even he sounded a cautiously optimistic note. Clinton, he said, had announced at the end of the meeting that "tomorrow we get down to the real s." That was Dole's polite abbreviation, not the president's. Kasich listened to all this with equal parts bemusement and concern. Now Armey was trying to read Clinton's body language! "Get anyone in that room and they change," Kasich thought to himself. And what was with Dole? Kasich could not tell. He could never tell. He liked Dole, he admired his coolness, but he was still a mystery. He knew nothing about the grand old man when the process started and felt that he knew even less about him now.

THERE were three more days of talks, from Saturday, January 6, through the following Tuesday, January 9, with Sunday off because of a massive snowstorm that hit Washington. When the Republicans came in with their spending bill Saturday, Clinton presented them the Daschle plan. With that little deal done, the government would reopen. It was all so simple and anticlimactic. For weeks the Republicans had pounded away on that one theme, demanding that the Democrats put down a seven-year budget scored by the CBO. From the Republican perspective, it was supposed to be a massive victory when and if that happened. White House strategists had known for weeks that they could present such a budget, and that when they did, it probably would have precisely the opposite effect than what the Republicans intended because of the way it was assembled. There was less given back in taxes and much less saved in Medicare, Medicaid, and discretionary domestic programs than the Republican blueprint. The Democratic argument from then on became: Okay, we've done that, and still not cut the entitlement programs drastically. Now what's the problem?

In a sense, the Democrats' ability to present a balanced plan moved the talks further apart. It more clearly underscored the serious ideological policy differences that separated the two sides. The Republicans came in with one final offer, based on the lowest numbers they could accept on Medicare cuts and tax cuts, taken from plans put together by Blue Dog conservative Democrats and a bipartisan Senate coalition. It was not the win the Democrats were looking for—not close. On Monday, the Republicans reworked the same numbers. Clinton and Gore kept saying: Here's an idea! What about this? But it was all headed nowhere. At the end of the Monday meeting the two sides broached the notion of exit strategies. Tuesday could be the end.

If ever there was a perfect metaphor for the entire frustrating, inconclusive end game, the scene at the White House on that Tuesday, January 9, certainly provided it. The Republicans came in coached by their staff and advisers Kasich and Domenici to cut off the talks clearly and cleanly if the Democrats would not budge. Clinton kept making small gestures, almost literally holding them in the room with hints and suggestions of movement. Armey was awed by the president's performance. Every time the Republicans showed the slightest indication that they were about to leave the room, Clinton reached out to them "like he was reaching out for a life preserver to keep his head afloat," Armey thought. Here's another way of looking at it, he would say. How about this idea? What if we . . . ?

Gingrich, Dole, and Armey left the Oval Office at one point to huddle with their support staff in the Roosevelt Room. It was clear to Kasich and Domenici that the White House was not moving, just fooling around with numbers. "Just go back in and say, Look, let's suspend talks," Kasich said.

"Yeah, I really think we should end this now," said Dole.

The trio of Republican leaders returned to the Oval Office, only to reappear in the Roosevelt Room a half hour later.

"We've recessed for a week," said Gingrich.

"You what?" Kasich asked, bewildered. "What planet do these guys visit when they get in that Oval Office?" he wondered to himself. Armey confessed that the word "recess" was his idea after Clinton and Panetta balked at the word "suspension," saying it might hurt the national interest to use such a strong word. "I said it would probably be better to go with "recess" because it would make the markets less nervous," Armey said. Kasich felt like shining a flashlight into Armey's eyes.

Panetta then arrived with his notebook and started reading out a list of directions for what everyone, including Republican staff members, was going to do and say. The staffs would continue to meet while the main talks were in recess, he said. The governors would keep working toward an agreement on Medicaid and welfare. The press secretaries would spread the word that they were making progress and were just taking a temporary recess.

Kasich, Domenici, and the Republican staff members were dumbstruck. Why was the White House calling the shots? Was Panetta going to order them to run laps around the White House? When Panetta left, the advisers turned to Gingrich. The speaker was suddenly struck by the notion that perhaps Clinton had charmed him one last time and rendered him indecisive. "I don't know why we keep doing it, either," he said. "We ought to just cut it off."

"You should have said that in the Oval Office," Dole said to Gingrich.

"You're right," said Gingrich. "Let's get Panetta back in here."

Panetta was called back into the room. "Look," said Gingrich. "Maybe we weren't clear enough in the room. Maybe we need to reconvene the room. After talking here, I don't think we can go out with the idea we are making great progress and keep working on it."

"Look, we've got to think about the country," said Panetta.

"Well, we just don't think these other meetings are of any purpose," said Gingrich.

"All right," said Panetta. "Why don't I just say we'll continue to meet and follow up and leave it at that? And we'll say 'recess' instead of 'suspend.' "

Gingrich relented. "Fine," he said.

On the ride back to the Capitol, Gingrich started thinking about how they could manage the government with no agreement, and how the Republicans could communicate their position to the country. When the entourage arrived in the Senate Press Gallery for a final press conference, no one could find Kasich. The balanced budget was his perhaps more than anyone's. It came out of his committee. It was propelled by his energy. And now it was over. Everyone was looking for Kasich. The "late John Kasich," as Dole teasingly called him, because he was always late for meetings.

Usually he was late because he had a million things on his mind. This time he was late because he wanted to be. In his mind he was back in the Fenton schoolyard of his childhood. He had played baseball all day and he was thirsty and it was the bottom of the last inning and he had battled all the way and he had argued long and hard over whether the ball was fair or foul and he could not stand the thought of losing. Had he failed or had Gingrich's revolution let him down? He wanted to be alone. He went for a walk. He felt empty.

Epilogue

ONE MORNING IN March, Newt Gingrich arrived in his office at a quarter to nine after swimming laps for a half-hour in the House Gym. His legislative work for the second year of his term as speaker was about to begin. He carried a briefcase full of papers outlining his strategy for 1996, distilled from a long retreat with his staff down in Atlanta and several days of meetings in Washington with his House leadership team. But now his attention was on lessons from the past. Everything seemed different from a year earlier. The phenomenon known as Newt was no longer the centrifugal force of American politics.

The network cameras were long gone. They had left in February to chase Bob Dole and the pack out on the campaign trail. Gingrich had avoided the presidential maneuvering at first, but voted for Dole in the Georgia primary and attached himself to the presumptive nominee from then on, declaring that he was happy to assume the role of "junior partner" in their relationship. When he said that, no one thought he was being needlessly humble. It was a matter of pragmatic politics. More than ever before, Gingrich's future would depend on how he got along with Dole. They had come a long way from the contentious days of the 1980s when Gingrich had dismissed the veteran senator as a "tax collector for the welfare state." During the course of the balanced budget battle, Gingrich had grown to respect Dole's stamina and strength. But could it be a true partnership? Dole might have appeared inert and unimaginative at times during 1995 in contrast to the whirligig Gingrich, but he knew how to play the game. Now he had the power.

There was, in any case, less talk of governing from Capitol Hill. The very word "revolution," while not censored from the Republican lexicon, had fallen into disuse, regarded in retrospect as a rhetorical mistake that overpromised and frightened the public. There still was no balanced budget, but neither were there calls to shut down the government in reprisal. Gingrich no longer assumed that President Clinton would cave under pressure and accommodate the Republican agenda. The Republican strategy instead was being built around the expectation of presidential vetoes. Legislative attacks on environmental laws and federal regulations were packed away, and even Tom DeLay talked about how they had bungled that effort by sounding extremist.

Newt had not shut up, but he was less promiscuous with his rhetoric. Instead of the daily news briefings of his first three months in power, he now met with the press infrequently. "Who needs them?" he said of news briefings on that March morning. "They are inherently adversarial and hostile." The constant barrage of news had made him a celebrity, just as Sonny Bono had predicted on the day of the swearing-in. Was it worth it? Gingrich equivocated on an answer. His first reply was no. His notoriety, his transformation into a symbol that could be attacked and mocked, was too high a price to pay. He had mishandled himself, he said. "We kept thinking it was a series of tactical problems that we could solve, when in fact we were in a different world and we didn't understand that." But Gingrich is a politician who has always sought attention. That is how he rose to power. He could not shed that part of his personality even if he wanted to. And he would never want to.

He boasted about how often his mug appeared on national television during the Grammy awards broadcast; the network kept promoting his appearance on the sitcom *Murphy Brown*. He noted that in January he had traveled to twenty-five cities and raised more than $3.2 million for the party. No speaker before him had been that sort of financial draw. Yes, Democrats hated him and independents might be cool to him, but the partisans still loved him. That is what being a celebrity is all about. They love you and hate you but they know who you are. Newt had become another product on the shelf of American consumerism. He had spent countless hours studying Coca-Cola, the marketing giant headquartered near his Atlanta-area congressional district, and now he could define his turbulent first year with a metaphor of success from the soft-drink world. Maybe seeing his poll numbers drop was the inevitable start-up cost of developing something new. Maybe the ups and downs of the revolution were unavoidable in seeking to capture a share of the market. "You can look at 1995," Newt Gingrich said, "as the sum cost of inventing Diet Coke."

Note on Sources

THIS BOOK IS based on more than three hundred interviews, as well as internal memos, calendars, diaries, and other primary documents. All the central figures were interviewed several times each. In many chapters, the method of sourcing is obvious and on the record. It is less apparent in the final two chapters, which provide an inside narrative account of the balanced budget negotiations. Every scene in those chapters is based on the recollections of at least two informants and supplemented by written notes and records whenever possible. The core of this book was first published in the *Washington Post* in an occassional series of articles between March 1995 and January 1996. In most cases, immediately before publication, the main characters in each story or their aides were read those sections in which they appeared. This was done solely in pursuit of accuracy. The authors and our editors maintained complete control over what was written. Most of the main interviews were tape-recorded. Arrangements are being made to house the tapes at the congressional research division of the National Archives.

House members interviewed most frequently for this work were John Kasich, Tom DeLay, John Boehner, Newt Gingrich, Dick Armey, Robert Livingston, Robert Walker, Cass Ballenger, Lindsey Graham, and Sam Brownback. Other House members interviewed included: Bill Barrett, Charles Bass, Sherwood

Boehlert, David Bonior, Sonny Bono, Steve Chabot, Dick Chrysler, Tom Coburn, Gary Condit, Christopher Cox, Frank Creamins, Duke Cunningham, Norman Dicks, Robert Ehrlich, Phil English, Mark Foley, Jon Fox, Barney Frank, Bob Franks, David Funderburk, Greg Ganske, Bill Goodling, Steve Gunderson, Dave Hobson, Pete Hoekstra, Tim Hutchinson, Ernest Istook, Dale Kildee, Steve Largent, Rick Lazio, Jerry Lewis, Jim Longley, David McIntosh, Buck McKeon, Don Manzullo, Dan Miller, George Miller, Susan Molinari, Sue Myrick, Mark Neumann, Charles Norwood, David Obey, Major Owens, Bill Paxon, Tom Petri, Earl Pomeroy, John Edward Porter, Frank Riggs, Pat Roberts, Marge Roukema, Charles Schumer, John Shadegg, Christopher Shays, Bud Shuster, Chris Smith, Lamar Smith, Linda Smith, Nick Smith, Mark Souder, Floyd Spence, Curt Weldon, Gerald Weller, and Roger Wicker.

Staff assistants for dozens of other congressmen and congressional committees were also interviewed. Leadership aides who were most helpful included Tony Blankley, Arne Christenson, Bruce Cuthbertson, Jim Dyer, John Feehery, Robert George, Ed Gillespie, Ralph Hellman, Barry Jackson, Bill Jarrell, Kerry Knott, Rick May, Leigh Ann Metzger, Dan Meyer, Gary Visscher, and Mildred Webber. Others who were interviewed and provided documents included Haley Barbour, chairman of the Republican National Committee, and his political lieutenant, Don Fierce; pollsters and advisers Linda DiVall, Frank Luntz, and Bill McInturff; and lobbyists David Rehr, Dan Mattoon, Bob Rusbuldt, Mark Isakowitz, and Steve Bell. Most helpful at the White House were senior assistant George Stephanopoulos and policy aide Gene Sperling.

Acknowledgments

THIS BOOK WOULD not have been possible without the freedom and encouragement provided us at the *Washington Post* by publisher Donald Graham, executive editor Leonard Downie, and managing editor Robert Kaiser. Karen DeYoung and Bill Hamilton, our editors on the National staff, gave us strong support and advice throughout the year that we spent rambling around inside Gingrich's revolution. Bob Barnes brought a clear, skillful eye to the editing of our series, and Maralee Schwartz kept us going with her enthusiasm and deep knowledge of congressional politics. As usual, it was comforting to know that Bob Woodward was around when we needed him. We are indebted to the work and wisdom of colleagues David Broder, Dan Morgan, Eric Pianin, E. J. Dionne, Mary McGrory, Dan Balz, John Yang, Kevin Merida, Guy Gugliotta, Peter Milius, Barbara Saffir, and Richard Cohen. A special nod to Valerie Strauss for supplying us with cinnamon and gossip. Thanks also to our *Post* podmates Schmitty, Pierre, and Serge for putting up with us.

It was Rafe Sagalyn, our friend and literary agent, along with Alice Mayhew, the incomparable Simon & Schuster editor, who envisioned this work being transformed into a book. Sarah Baker at Touchstone, whose voice lifted us every time she called, helped make it a reality. Thanks also to Ann Adelman, a first-rate copy editor, and to Sue Fleming and Jennifer Swihart in Publicity.

David Maraniss kept going only because of the love and nurturing of his wife Linda, his kids Andrew and Sarah, and the rest of his family, Elliott and Mary Maraniss, Jim Maraniss, Wendy Maraniss, and Jean Alexander. Michael Weisskopf owes everything to the spiritual leaders of his revolution, wife Judith and son Skyler, whose love and humor were sustaining, and to the lifetime cheerleading of his clan: Jack and Marcella Stillerman; Richard and Martha Weisskopf; Michael, Leslie, Warren, and Bennie Flesch; and Sabina Katz.

For the most part, Newt Gingrich and the House Republicans were open all year long as they operated with two nosy reporters in their midst, letting us back time and again even when our reports stung them. We are especially grateful for our frequent audiences with the Pope of McKees Rocks, who gave us an extra bounce with his rollicking sense of humor and exuberance for life.

Index